"十三五"全国高等院校民航服务专业规划教材

民航客舱 服务英语教程

主　编◎李雯艳　王　莹
副主编◎刘媛媛　王盈秋

Civil Aviation Cabin Service English

清华大学出版社
北京

内 容 简 介

本教材是按照空中乘务员客舱服务工作流程设计和编写的,旨在使学生在模拟实际工作的情景中,练习并掌握原汁原味的客舱服务用语,能够用英语与客舱乘客友好交流,并提供优质的服务。

本教材可作为空中乘务专业本(专)科学生的课堂教学用书,也可以作为民航企业及各培训机构的空乘人员岗前培训教材,亦可作为具有一定英语基础的旅客的自学用书等。

图书在版编目(CIP)数据

民航客舱服务英语教程/李雯艳,王莹主编 . —北京:清华大学出版社,2018(2024.2重印)
("十三五"全国高等院校民航服务专业规划教材)
ISBN 978-7-302-49052-4

Ⅰ.①民…　Ⅱ.①李…②王…　Ⅲ.①民用航空－旅客运输－商业服务－英语－高等学校－教材
Ⅳ.①F560.9

中国版本图书馆 CIP 数据核字(2017)第 295505 号

责任编辑:杜春杰
封面设计:刘　超
版式设计:楠竹文化
责任校对:王　颖
责任印制:丛怀宇

出版发行:清华大学出版社
　　　　网　　　址:https://www.tup.com.cn,https://www.wqxuetang.com
　　　　地　　　址:北京清华大学学研大厦 A 座　邮　　　编:100084
　　　　社 总 机:010-83470000　邮　　　购:010-62786544
　　　　投稿与读者服务:010-62776969,c-service@tup.tsinghua.edu.cn
　　　　质量反馈:010-62772015,zhiliang@tup.tsinghua.edu.cn
　　　　课件下载:https://www.tup.com.cn,010-62788903

印 装 者:三河市天利华印刷装订有限公司
经　　销:全国新华书店
开　　本:185mm×260mm　印　张:11.25　字　　数:265 千字
版　　次:2018 年 6 月第 1 版　印　　次:2024 年 2 月第 7 次印刷
定　　价:35.00 元

产品编号:077346-01

"十三五"全国高等院校民航服务专业规划教材
丛书主编及专家指导委员会

丛 书 总 主 编　刘永(北京中航未来科技集团有限公司董事长兼总裁)

丛 书 副 总 主 编　马晓伟(北京中航未来科技集团有限公司常务副总裁)

丛 书 副 总 主 编　郑大地(北京中航未来科技集团有限公司教学副总裁)

丛 书 总 主 审　朱益民(原海南航空公司总裁、原中国货运航空公司总裁、原上海航空公司总裁)

丛 书 总 顾 问　沈泽江(原中国民用航空华东管理局局长)

丛 书 总 执 行 主 编　王益友[江苏民航职业技术学院(筹)院长、教授]

丛 书 总 航 空 法 律 顾 问　程颖(荷兰莱顿大学国际法研究生、全国高职高专"十二五"规划教材《航空法规》主审)

丛书专家指导委员会主任

关云飞(长沙航空职业技术学院教授)

张树生(国务院津贴获得者,山东交通学院教授)

刘岩松(沈阳航空航天大学教授)

姚宝(上海外国语大学教授)

李剑峰(山东大学教授)

张威(沈阳师范大学教授)

成积春(曲阜师范大学教授)

万峻池(美术评论家、著名美术品收藏家)

"十三五"全国高等院校民航服务专业规划教材编委会

出 版 说 明

随着经济的稳步发展,我国已经进入经济新常态的阶段,特别是十九大指出:中国社会主要矛盾已经转化为人民日益增长的美好生活需要和不平衡不充分的发展之间的矛盾,这客观上要求社会服务系统要完善升级。作为公共交通运输的主要组成部分,民航运输在满足人们对美好生活追求和促进国民经济发展中扮演着重要的角色,具有广阔的发展空间。特别是"十三五"期间,国家高度重视民航业的发展,将民航业作为推动我国经济社会发展的重要战略产业,预示着我国民航业将会有更好、更快的发展。从国产化飞机 C919 的试飞,到宽体飞机规划的出台,以及民航发展战略的实施,标志着我国民航业已经步入崭新的发展阶段,这一阶段的特点是以人才为核心,而这一发展模式必将进一步对民航人才质量提出更高的要求。面对民航业发展对人才培养提出的挑战,培养服务于民航业发展的高质量人才,不仅需要转变人才培养观念,创新教育模式,更需要加强人才培养过程中基本环节的建设,而教材建设就是其首要的任务。

我国民航服务专业的学历教育,经过 18 年的探索与发展,其办学水平、办学结构、办学规模、办学条件和师资队伍等方面都发生了巨大的变化,专业建设水平稳步提高,适应民航发展的人才培养体系初步形成。但我们应该清醒地看到,目前我国民航服务类专业的人才培养仍存在着诸多问题,特别是专业人才培养质量仍不能适应民航发展对人才的需求,人才培养的规模与高质量人才短缺的矛盾仍很突出。而目前相关专业教材的开发还处于探索阶段,缺乏系统性与规范性。已出版的民航服务类专业教材,在吸收民航服务类专业研究成果方面做出了有益的尝试,涌现出不同层次的系列教材,推动了民航服务的专业建设与人才培养,但从总体来看,民航服务类教材的建设仍落后于民航业对专业人才培养的实践要求,教材建设已成为相关人才培养的瓶颈。这就需要以引领和服务专业发展为宗旨,系统总结民航服务实践经验与教学研究成果,开发全面反映民航服务职业特点、符合人才培养规律和满足教学需要的系统性专业教材,以积极、有效地推进民航服务专业人才的培养工作。

基于上述思考,编委会经过两年多的实际调研与反复论证,在广泛征询民航业内专家的意见与建议、总结我国民航服务类专业教育的研究成果后,结合我国民航服务业的发展趋势,致力于编写出一套系统的、具有一定权威性和实用性的民航服务类系列教材,为推进我国民航服务人才的培养尽微薄之力。

本系列教材由沈阳航空航天大学、南昌航空大学、郑州航空工业管理学院、上海民航职业技术学院、长沙航空职业技术学院、西安航空职业技术学院、中原工学院、上海外国语大学、山东大学、大连外国语大学、沈阳师范大学、曲阜师范大学、湖南艺术职业学院、陕西师范大学、兰州大学、云南大学、四川大学、湖南民族职业学院、江西青年职业学院、天津交通职业学院、潍坊职业学院、南京旅游职业学院等多所高校的众多资深专家和学者共同打造,还邀请了多名原中国东方航空公司、原中国南方航空公司、原中国国际航空公司和原海南航空公司中从事多年乘务工作的乘务长和乘务员参与教材的编写。

目前,我国民航服务类的专业教育呈现着多元化、多层次的办学格局,各类学校的办学模式也呈现出个性化的特点,在人才培养体系、课程设置以及课程内容等方面,各学校之间存在着一定的差异,对教材也有不同的需求。为了能够更好地满足不同办学层次、教学模式对教材的需要,本套教材主要突出以下特点。

第一,兼顾本、专科不同培养层次的教学需要。鉴于近些年我国本科层次民航服务专业办学规模的不断扩大,在教材需求方面显得十分迫切,同时,专科层面的办学已经到了规模化的阶段,完善与更新教材体系和内容迫在眉睫,本套教材充分考虑了各类办学层次的需要,本着"求同存异、个性单列、内容升级"的原则,通过教材体系的科学架构和教材内容的层次化,以达到兼顾民航服务类本、专科不同层次教学之需要。

第二,将最新实践经验和专业研究成果融入教材。服务类人才培养是系统性问题,具有很强的内在规定性,民航服务的实践经验和专业建设成果是教材的基础,本套教材以丰富理论、培养技能为主,力求夯实服务基础、培养服务职业素质,将实践层面行之有效的经验与民航服务类人才培养规律的研究成果有效融合,以提高教材对人才培养的有效性。

第三,落实素质教育理念,注重服务人才培养。习近平总书记在党的十九大报告中强调,"要全面贯彻党的教育方针,落实立德树人根本任务,发展素质教育,推进教育公平,培养德智体美全面发展的社会主义建设者和接班人",人才以德为先,以社会主义价值观铸就人的灵魂,才能使人才担当重任,也是高校人才培养的基本任务。教育实践表明,素质是人才培养的基础,也是人才职业发展的基石,人才的能力与技能以精神与灵魂为附着,但在传统的民航服务教材体系中,包含素质教育板块的教材较为少见。根据党的教育方针,本套教材的编写考虑到素质教育与专业能力培养的关系,以及素质对职业生涯的潜在影响,首次在我国民航服务专业教学中提出专业教育与人文素质并重、素质决定能力的培养理念,以独特的视野,精心打造素质教育教材板块,使教材体系更加系统,强化了教材特色。

第四,必要的服务理论与专业能力培养并重。调研分析表明,忽视服务理论与人文素质所培养出的人才很难有宽阔的职业胸怀与职业精神,其未来的职业生涯发展就会乏力。因此,教材不应仅是对单纯技能的阐述与训练指导,更应该是不淡化专业能力培养的同时,强化行业知识、职业情感、服务机理、职业道德等关系到职业发展潜力的要素的培养,以期培养出高层次和高质量的民航服务人才。

第五,架构适合未来发展需要的课程体系与内容。民航服务具有很强的国际化特点,而我国民航服务的思想、模式与方法也正处于不断创新的阶段,紧紧把握未来民航服务的发展趋势,提出面向未来的解决问题的方案,是本套教材的基本出发点和应该承担的责任。我们力图将未来民航服务的发展趋势、服务思想、服务模式创新、服务理论体系以及服务管理等内容进行重新架构,以期能对我国民航服务人才培养,乃至整个民航服务业的发展起到引领作用。

第六,扩大教材的种类,使教材的选择更加宽泛。鉴于我国目前尚缺乏民航服务专业更高层次办学模式的规范,各学校的人才培养方案各具特点,差异明显,为了使教材更适合于办学的需要,本套教材打破了传统教材的格局,通过课程分割、内容优化和课外外延化等方式,增加了教材体系的课程覆盖面,使不同办学层次、关联专业,可以通过教材合理组合获得完整的专业教材选择机会。

　　本套教材规划出版品种大约为四十种,分为:① 人文素养类教材,包括《大学语文》《应用文写作》《艺术素养》《跨文化沟通》《民航职业修养》《中国传统文化》等。② 语言类教材,包括《民航客舱服务英语教程》《民航客舱实用英语口语教程》《民航实用英语听力教程》《民航播音训练》《机上广播英语》《民航服务沟通技巧》等。③ 专业类教材,包括《民航概论》《民航服务概论》《中国民航常飞客源国概况》《民航危险品运输》《客舱安全管理与应急处置》《民航安全检查技术》《民航服务心理学》《航空运输地理》《民航服务法律实务与案例教程》等。④ 职业形象类教材,包括《空乘人员形体与仪态》《空乘人员职业形象设计与化妆》《民航体能训练》等。⑤ 专业特色类教材,包括《民航服务手语训练》《空乘服务专业导论》《空乘人员求职应聘面试指南》《民航面试英语教程》等。

　　为了开发职业能力,编者联合有关 VR 开发公司开发了一些与教材配套的手机移动端VR 互动资源,学生可以利用这些资源体验真实场景。

　　本套教材是迄今为止民航服务类专业较为完整的教材系列之一,希望能借此为我国民航服务人才的培养,乃至我国民航服务水平的提高贡献力量。民航发展方兴未艾,民航教育任重道远,为民航服务事业发展培养高质量的人才是各类人才培养部门的共同责任,相信集民航教育的业内学者、专家之共同智慧,凝聚有识之士心血的这套教材的出版,对加速我国民航服务专业建设、完善人才培养模式、优化课程体系、丰富教学内容,以及加强师资队伍建设能起到一定的推动作用。在教材使用的过程中,我们真诚地希望听到业内专家、学者批评的声音,收到广大师生的反馈意见,以利于进一步提高教材的水平。

　　客服信箱:thjdservice@126.com。

丛书序

《礼记·学记》曰："古之王者,建国君民,教学为先。"教育是兴国安邦之本,决定着人类的今天,也决定着人类的未来,企业发展也大同小异,重视人才是企业的成功之道,别无二选。航空经济是现代经济发展的新趋势,是当今世界经济发展的新引擎,民航是经济全球化的主流形态和主导模式,是区域经济发展和产业升级的驱动力。作为发展中的中国民航业,有巨大的发展潜力,其民航发展战略的实施必将成为我国未来经济发展的增长点。

"十三五"期间正值实现我国民航强国战略构想的关键时期,"一带一路"倡议方兴未艾,"空中丝路"越来越宽阔。面对高速发展的民航运输,需要推动持续的创新与变革;同时,基于民航运输的安全性和规范性的特点,其对人才有着近乎苛刻的要求,只有人才培养先行,夯实人才基础,才能抓住国家战略转型与产业升级的巨大机遇,实现民航运输发展的战略目标。经历多年民航服务人才发展的积累,我国建立了较为完善的民航服务人才培养体系,培养了大量服务民航发展的各类人才,保证了我国民航运输业的高速持续发展。与此同时,我国民航人才培养正面临新的挑战,既要通过教育创新,提升人才品质,又需要在人才培养过程中精细化,把人才培养目标落实到人才培养的过程中,而教材作为专业人才培养的基础,需要先行,从而发挥引领作用。教材建设发挥的作用并不局限于专业教育本身,其对行业发展的引领,专业人才的培养方向,人才素质、知识、能力结构的塑造以及职业发展潜力的培养具有不可替代的作用。

我国民航运输发展的实践表明,人才培养决定着民航发展的水平,而民航人才的培养需要社会各方面的共同努力。我们惊喜地看到,清华大学出版社秉承"自强不息,厚德载物"的人文精神,发挥强势的品牌优势,投身到民航服务专业系列教材的开发行列,改变了民航服务教材研发的格局,体现了其对社会责任的担当。

本套教材体系组织严谨,精心策划,高屋建瓴,深入浅出,具有突出的特色。第一,从民航服务人才培养的全局出发,关注了民航服务产业的未来发展趋势,架构了以培养目标为导向的教材体系与内容结构,比较全面地反映了服务人才培养趋势,具有良好的统领性;第二,很好地回归了教材的本质——适用性,体现在每本教材均有独特的视角和编写立意,既有高度的提升、理论的升华,也注重教育要素在课程体系中的细化,具有较强的可用性;第三,引入了职业素质教育的理念,补齐了服务人才素质教育缺少教材的短板,可谓是对传统服务人才培养理念的一次冲击;第四,教材编写人员参与面非常广泛。这反映出本套教材充分体现了当今民航服务专业教育的教学成果和编写者的思考,形成了相互交流的良性机制,势必对全国民航服务类专业的发展起到推动作用。

教材建设是专业人才培养的基础,与其服务的行业的发展交互作用,共同实现人才培养—社会检验的良性循环是助推民航服务人才的动力。希望这套教材能够在民航服务类专业人才培养的实践中,发挥更广泛的积极作用。相信通过不断总结与完善,这套教材一定会成为具有自身特色的、适应我国民航业发展要求的,以及深受读者喜欢的规范教材。

此为序。

原海南航空公司总裁、原中国货运航空公司总裁、原上海航空公司总裁

朱益民

2017 年 9 月

前　言

近年来，我国对外交往规模日渐扩大，越来越多的外籍人士出现在民航工作环境中，这就不仅要求乘务人员具备基本的对外交往和用英语交流的能力，而且还要能够以英语为媒介来处理一些客舱服务的基本问题。因此，以提高乘务员英语综合水准为目的的教材就成为发展的趋势。本教材与其他教材相比，更侧重客舱服务的职业性、实用性和系统性。

一、编写思路

本教材以培养职业能力为核心、以工作实践为主线、以学习情景为主体、以客舱服务工作过程为基点编写，使学生在了解乘务工作专业知识的背景下，能够熟练掌握并应用英语与客舱乘客友好交流，提供优质的服务。

二、教材特色

本教材的特色主要体现在"全面性""实用性""专业性"和"生动性"等几个方面，通过本教材的学习，学生可以学有所用、学以致用、以用促学、学用统一。教材特色具体体现如下。

1. 全面性

本教材涵盖了乘务员客舱服务的所有流程，包括航前准备、迎客、机上安检、延误、客舱餐饮服务、特殊旅客服务、客舱应急程序、客舱娱乐服务、转机服务、免税品销售、入境卡的填写及降落前和降落后等主要环节。

2. 实用性

本教材采用地道的、原汁原味的英语，向使用者提供大量的客舱口语和广播词训练素材，并充分考虑到语言的得体性、可接受性以及文化的多样性。会话部分情景生动逼真，又辅助有富于创意的并符合行业情景的角色扮演，使学生能够进一步巩固和发展他们的语言交际能力。

3. 专业性

本教材在编写过程中随时请教资深的民航服务工作人士，同时结合了本人多年的乘务英语教学经验，使教材具备了专业性和职业性的特点。

4. 生动性

本人在多年的一线教学里收集了一些客舱服务的趣味素材编写到本书中，使本书可以达到寓教于乐，活跃课堂气氛，充分调动学生的积极性的目的，使学生在学习知识的同时又不失乐趣。

三、教材结构及内容

本教材共 12 个单元，每单元由四大部分组成：Dialogues（对话）、Announcements（广播词）、Supplementary Reading（课外阅读）和 Interview English（面试英语）。每单元课时建议分配如下：

单元	标题	课时
1	Preparation for the Flight	10
2	Passenger Reception	8
3	Safety Check before Take-off	8
4	Reasons for Delay	8
5	Drink and Meal Service	10
6	Special Passengers Service	8
7	Emergency Procedures	8
8	In-Flight Entertainment	8
9	Duty Free Sales	8
10	Transfer Service	8
11	Customs，Immigration and Quarantine	8
12	Pre-arrival and Post-arrival	10
合计	12 个单元	102 课时

教师可以按教学进展情况灵活掌握讲授方法和进度，其中 Supplementary Reading 部分可以由教师指导学生课外阅读，不建议占用过多课堂时间。

四、使用说明

本书由李雯艳老师，王莹老师担任主编；刘媛媛老师，王盈秋老师担任副主编。具体编写分工如下：每章的 Section A，Section B，Section D 和练习答案部分由李雯艳老师编写；每章的 Section C 由刘媛媛老师编写；王盈秋老师统稿；王莹老师主审。

文中图片大多数取自于互联网相关网站，特此鸣谢。由于编者水平有限，加之时间仓促，书中也许会出现一些不足之处，恳请同行及读者不吝赐教。

编者

2017 年 7 月

CONTENTS 目录

Unit 1
Preparation for the Flight

Lead-in questions

1. What does the purser need to do before the briefing?

2. What should flight attendants do before the passengers board the aircraft?

3. What do they usually discuss at the preflight briefing?

Section A   Dialogues

Dialogue one

Setting：The purser is having the preflight briefing.
(CF＝chief purser，FA＝flight attendant，PS＝purser)

CF：Good afternoon，everyone. Let's begin our briefing. I'm your chief purser and my name is Shirley. Nice to meet you!

FA:Nice to meet you,too.

CF:Now let's look at today's flight route. We will head for New York. FA1,would you like to tell us some information about this flight?

FA1:Yes,the departure time is 14:30,the arrival time is _____,and the estimated flight time is _____ .

CF:Thank you. FA2,can you tell me the weather condition in New York?

FA2:Well,it is sunny in New York. The temperature rises to 28℃ and drops to 19℃.

CF:Thanks a lot. FA4,can you tell me the airplane type and the passenger loading?

FA4:The airplane type is Boeing 777. Passenger loading will be 9 in first class and 240 in economy class.

CF:Thank you FA4. PS,would you like to give a short briefing?

PS:Sure. Firstly, please check the equipment which you must bring in your tool-kit. Secondly,please pay attention to the details in service. For example,keep some meals for those passengers who are sleeping during the flight and you aren't able to wake them up. Lastly,pay attention to the special passengers such as VIP,UM,CIP,senior,infant, disabled person and passengers who have ordered special meal,etc.

CF:Thanks a lot,and hope that we will cooperate with each other as a team. Have a good journey.

Dialogue two

Setting:

(*The purser assigns the task and asks the flight attendant to have a preflight check for the coming flight.*)

PS:Good morning,everyone. Now I will assign the task by seniority and qualification for the coming flight. I will take first class with Miss Liu. The rest of you will be in economy class. Ms Li,would you please check the entertainment system to see if they are functional? Including call button,video and audio,reading light and loudspeaker.

FA:Sure.

PS:Miss Bai,please check emergency equipment. Would you tell us what you should check?

FA:Ok. I should check fire extinguishers, first-aid kits, life vests, oxygen masks, megaphones and life rafts.

PS:Mr. Wu,would you please check the galley and the lavatory?

FA:No problem. I will check oven,water heater,drink and food in the galley. Next,I will make sure the lavatory amenities are in position and sufficient,waste bins are clean,and the flush buttons work.

PS:Well,please check them with care. Miss Liu,would you please help me check the cabin to see if the items in the seat pocket are in correct sequence, the seat belts are crossed, the tables are stowed, armrests are down, all the window shades are up and all overhead bins remain open?

FA: I'm pleased to do it.

PS: Thank you for your cooperation.

Words and Expressions

purser /ˈpəːsə/	n.	乘务长
flight attendant		空乘
preflight briefing		航前准备会
first class		头等舱
economy class		经济舱
equipment /iˈkwipmənt/	n.	设备,装备
senior /ˈsiːniə/	a.	较年长者
infant /ˈinfənt/	n.	婴儿;幼儿;未成年人
assign /əˈsaɪn/	v.	分配;指派
seniority /siːniˈɒrɪtɪ/	n.	资历;年长
qualification /ˌkwɒlifiˈkeɪʃən/	n.	资格;条件
entertainment /entəˈteinmənt/	n.	娱乐;消遣
functional /ˈfʌŋkʃənəl/	a.	功能的
loudspeaker /laʊdˈspiːkə/	n.	扬声器
emergency /iˈməːdʒənsi/	n.	突发事件;紧急情况
fire extinguisher		灭火器
first-aid kit		急救箱
life vest		救生衣
oxygen mask		氧气面罩
megaphone /ˈmegəfəʊn/	n.	扩音器,喇叭筒
life raft		救生筏
galley /ˈgæli/	n.	厨房
lavatory /ˈlævətəri/	n.	厕所
amenities /əˈmiːnətiz/	n.	便利设施
sufficient /səˈfiʃənt/	a.	足够的;充分的
sequence /ˈsiːkwəns/	n.	序列;顺序
armrest /ˈaːmrest/	n.	扶手
cooperation /kəʊˌɒpəˈreɪʃən/	n.	合作,协作

Exercises

1. Questions for discussion.

1) What should pre-flight preparations cover prior to the boarding of passengers?

2) What should you check if the purser asks you to check the emergency equipment?

3) What should you check if the purser asks you to check the entertainment system?

4) What's the main task working as a flight attendant?

5) Can you explain the operation of fire extinguisher?

2. Oral practice.

Work with a partner to make up the following dialogues. Situational settings are as follows.

1) Today you are the chief purser, you are going to have a preflight briefing.

2) The flight attendants discuss the flight information and passenger's information at the preflight briefing.

Section B   Announcements

Check-in Announcements

Ladies and gentlemen,

Attention, please. The check-in counter for Flight CZ2867 bound for New York will be closed in forty minutes. Passengers who have not gone through check-in formalities, please go to the check-in counter as soon as possible. Thank you for your cooperation.

We hope you will enjoy your flight with China Southern Airlines. Thank you.

Ground Announcements

Ladies and gentlemen,

May I have your attention, please? Flight HX878 will take off in fifteen minutes. All passengers for this flight please go to gate 56 and board the aircraft immediately. Thank you!

Words and expressions

check-in counter		办理登机手续的柜台
bound for		开往
go through		办理;完成
formality /fɔː'mæləti/	*n.*	正式手续

Exercises

1. Match the English phrases in column A with the Chinese translations in column B.

A	B
(　) a. chief purser	1) 头等舱
(　) b. Air New Zealand (NZ)	2) 灭火器
(　) c. first class	3) 尼泊尔皇家航空公司

(　　　) d. preflight briefing 　　　　　4）特殊旅客

(　　　) e. special passenger 　　　　　5）经济舱

(　　　) f. fire extinguisher 　　　　　6）航前准备会议

(　　　) g. first-aid kit 　　　　　　　7）娱乐系统

(　　　) h. entertainment system 　　　8）主任乘务长

(　　　) i. economy class 　　　　　　9）新西兰航空公司

(　　　) j. Royal Nepal Airlines (RA) 　10）急救包

2. Translate the following sentences into English.

1）我们现在开航前准备会,我是本次航班的主任乘务长。

2）谁能告诉我头等舱和经济舱分别有多少乘客?

3）很高兴今天能与各位一起工作。

4）我们既然是个团队,那么在整个飞行过程中就应该互相配合。

5）飞行距离是 5 600 千米,飞行时间大约是 7 小时。

6）北京和纽约存在时差,请注意调整。

7）我是本次航班的乘务长玛丽,我谨代表中国国际航空有限公司欢迎您搭乘我们从北京飞往伦敦的 CA873 号航班。

8）乘务员的主要职责就是确保飞机和机上所有乘客的安全。

9）一名称职的乘务员必须要有崇高的目标和激情。

10）我和皮特负责头等舱和商务舱,其他人负责经济舱。

3. Translate the following sentences into Chinese.

1）Operate the selector lever according to the regulations and be sure to make cross check.

2）Now let's get to know each other. Please raise your hand when I call your name.

3）We should leave the passengers a very good first impression with our sweet smile when they board the plane.

4）Please help me to check the entertainment system to see if they are functional.

5）Please keep some meals for those passengers who are asleep during the flight and you should not wake them up.

6）Based on the flight service regulations, we will serve lunch at about 12：00 o'clock, not right after the beverage service.

7）It's time to turn off the boarding music and welcome passengers board the plane.

8）For a flight attendant, there is a great deal to do to prepare for the flight even before they board the aircraft.

9）Please check the emergency equipment after boarding and report to your purser.

10）The ground temperature rises to 34℃ and drops to 19℃.

4. The cabin crew greet each other at the preflight briefing. Please fill in the blanks of the following dialogue.

(PS＝purser, FA＝flight attendant)

PS：Ladies and gentlemen, may I have your attention please? Now let's begin our preflight briefing. I am the purser of today's flight. My name is Li Ying. Nice to meet you!

FAS：(1)_____.

PS：Would you please introduce each other?

FA1：(2)_____.

PS：Glad to meet you, too. Next one, please.

FA2：(3)_____.

PS：How do you do? Next one, please.

FA3：(4)_____.

PS：I am pleased to know you. The last one, please.

FA4：(5)_____.

PS：Today I am very happy to work with you. Hope to have a good trip. Thank you very much.

5. Fill in the blanks in the following sentences with the words given below. Change the form where necessary.

counter   senior   remain   assign   sufficient
qualification   cooperation   check   equipment   estimate

1) Will there be _____ stocks to meet our demand?

2) We _____ the cost to be four thousand dollars.

3) We should not set light by the advice of our _____.

4) There is need to _____ the accuracy of these figures.

5) They had every _____ for success.

6) He _____ in the hospital for a whole month.

7) _____ and technology upgrades cann't solve the problem either.

8) When I taught, I would _____ a topic to children which they would write about.

9) They were sitting on stools at the _____ having coffee.

10) While in the past we stressed aid, now we stress economic _____.

6. Complete the paragraph with the correct word in the box.

patient   qualified   provide   aware   fluently
responsibility   safety   communicate   important   regards

As a flight attendant you should be well 1)_____ of your duties, that is, to play your part as a crew member and team member, especially with 2)_____ to safety, and to 3) _____ service straight from the heart to the best of your ability. All passengers' 4) _____ on board is the crew's most important 5) _____ . A 6) _____ crew must be responsible and 7) _____ . But that's not enough. High level of professionalism and hard working altitude are a must. Language is 8) _____ , too. A good flight attendant can 9) _____ with passengers who are not sharing the same language in English 10) _____ .

Section C   Supplementary Reading

Preparation for the Flight

Most people think flight attendants just do catering services. They are totally wrong. The truth is that they have much more to do, most of which passengers may not see. They need to do a lot of preparations before passengers get on board.

First, they are supposed to confirm schedule and do online exercises.

After checking the duty, flight attendants can confirm （确认）their duty online or by phone. It is important to make sure of the duty. In addition, flight attendants need to do online exercises before flights. The exercises are usually about cabin service requirements, emergency procedures, and so on.

Second, they need to read cabin notices.

It is also important for flight attendants to read cabin notices because they must know and learn the newest information about their duty and some new work requirements so that they can perform their duty better on flights.

Third, preflight briefings are required before each flight.

Flight attendants must attend preflight briefings before each flight. Usually, the preflight briefing will last for about half an hour. During the preflight briefing, each crew member will get to know each other first. Then, the purser will assign positions, make requirements for cabin service and safety, and lead flight attendants to review the emergency procedures. The security guard will also make requirements for safety.

Lastly, flight attendants make all the onboard preparations.

After the preflight briefing, the flight attendants get on board together. The first thing is to check the emergency equipment. Then they count the number of food and drinks. After that, they also prepare service items such as blankets, headsets, newspaper and so on. These preparations usually last for about half an hour. Then, they wait for the passengers to come and serve them.

Questions for discussion.

1. How do flight attendants confirm their duty?

2. Are flights attendants required to read cabin notices each flight? Why or why not?

3. Why are preflight briefings required before each flight?

4. What service items should be checked?

5. What else do you think flight attendants should prepare before flight, besides preparations mentioned in the passage?

Section D   Interview English

Daily hot topics:

Self- introduction

The typical questions on daily hot topics.

1. What's your name?

2. How old are you?

3. Where are you from?

4. Would you tell me something about your family?

5. What are your outstanding qualities and your greatest weakness?

The following question has been usually asked when you have an interview. There is an example. The answer is given for your reference.

Could you make a self-introduction?

I'm No. 15. I'm twenty-two years old. I was born in _____ . I graduated from _____ . There are three people in my family, my father, my mother and I. My parents love me very much and I love them just as much. We live a happy life together. I'm always positive, friendly and patient to people around me. I like to get along with different people, so I'm easy-going and sometimes very humorous. I like cleaning my house very much. I can't bear dirtiness. Maybe my greatest weakness is too clean. I like reading, listening to music and traveling.

Role-play practice:

You want to be a flight attendant and have an interview. You are asked to make a brief self-introduction. Please have an interview role-play with your partner.

Unit 2
Passenger Reception

Lead-in questions

1. What is your opinion of how to become a qualified flight attendant?
2. What do you think of the job as a flight attendant?
3. What do flight attendants need to do during the flight?

Section A   Dialogues

Dialogue one

Setting: *The passengers are boarding the plane. A flight attendant named Mary is standing at the front cabin door to welcome the passengers aboard. At this time an old lady seems lost in the cabin. Mary comes up to her.*

(P:passenger)

Mary:Good morning. Welcome aboard! What can I do for you,Madam?

P1:Good morning. Er...it is the first time for me to take a plane. I don't know where my seat is?

Mary:May I see your boarding pass,please?

P1:Sure. Here you are!

Mary:The seat number is 54A. Well,it's in the last row of the cabin, a window seat. I'd like to show you your seat.

P1:It's very nice of you.

Mary:Could I help you carry your rucksack?

P1:No,thank you. I can do it by myself.

(*When they get there,however,they find that the seat has been occupied by a man*)

Mary:(to the man)Excuse me,Sir. May I see your boarding card?

P2:Yes. Here you are!

Mary:Thank you! I'm afraid you're sitting in the wrong seat. This is 54A,yet your seat number is 45A. The seat number is shown along the edge of the overhead rack.

P2:Oh,I'm very sorry. Today I feel a little dizzy so I didn't see it clearly. I move at once.

Mary:Do you need my help?

P2:Um...yes,I don't know where I should put my overcoat. It's creased putting in the overhead rack. I don't want to hold it in my hand yet.

Mary:May I keep it for you? I'd like to hang it in the wardrobe.

P2:Sure. Thanks a lot.

Mary:By the way,is there anything valuable in the pockets?

P2:No,there isn't.

Mary:May I have your boarding card for later identification?

P2:Sure. That's very kind of you.

Mary:It's my pleasure.

(*Mary comes up to an over-wing exit. She talks to the passenger sitting next to the over-wing exit.*)

Mary:Excuse me,Miss. You are sitting next to an emergency exit.

P3:Oh,is it different from other seats?

Mary:Yeah,in the event of an emergency,you should open the exit according to the instructions of the captain.

P3:Wow,I'm afraid I can't assist you. You see I'm too slim to open the door. Furthermore, I've never done it before.

Mary:Well,would you mind sitting somewhere else? I can exchange it for you.

P3:Really? Very nice! Thank you.

Mary：Excuse me, Sir. Would you like to change your seat for one next to the emergency exit?

P4：Well. I'd like to.

Mary：Please don't touch the red handle. We need your help in case of emergency. Please read this instruction.

P4：No problem. I'd sat here before. I know what I should do.

Mary：Very Nice. Thank you, Sir.

Dialogue two

Setting：A young lady wants to sit with her son so she asks for a flight attendant named Jack's help.

P1：Excuse me, Sir. Do you mind if I ask for your help?

Jack：Of course not. It's our duty to serve you well.

P1：I want to sit together with my son in 15B. Could you help me to change a seat?

Jack：Well, follow me, please. Let me try to talk with the man beside your son to change seats with you.

Jack：(to that man) May I trouble you for a moment, Sir? This young lady would like to sit next to her son beside you. The boy is a little young so he should be taken care of. Would you mind exchanging seats with her?

P2：No, I wouldn't.

Jack：Thank you, and sorry for the trouble.

P2：Never mind.

Jack：The young lady's seat is in 16A. You can sit there.

P2：Ok.

(When Jack looks around, he finds a big luggage is put on the aisle next to the emergency exit.)

Jack：Excuse me, whose trunk is it?

P3：Er…It's mine. I can't find a proper place for it. It's too big to put into the overhead compartment or under the seat so I have to put here.

Jack：Oh, it's really very big! You know, luggage can not be left here as the aisle next to the emergency exit mustn't be blocked.

P3：Would you like to help me?

Jack：Well, if you'd like to let me keep it, I'll put it in the front cabin.

P3：Ok, you should keep it with care as there is a video camera in it.

Jack：I suggest you'd better take it with you in case it's broken.

P3：Okay, I take it out and keep it by myself.

Jack：Thank you for your understanding. By the way, please don't forget to take it with you when you deplane.

 P3：Thank you for your help.

 Jack：You are welcome.

Words and Expressions

boarding pass/card		登机卡
rucksack /ˈrʌkˌsæk/	n.	背包
overhead rack		舱顶行李架
dizzy /ˈdizi/	a.	头昏眼花的
crease /kriːs/	v.	弄皱
wardrobe /ˈwɔːdrəub/	n.	衣柜
valuable /ˈvæljuəbl/	a.	珍贵的
identification /aiˌdentifiˈkeiʃən/	n.	确认，鉴定
over-wing exit		机翼上方的紧急出口，逃生口
emergency exit		紧急出口
handle /ˈhænd(ə)l/	n.	把手，柄
	v.	处理；操作
luggage /ˈlʌgidʒ/	n.	行李
compartment /kəmˈpɑːtmənt/	n.	行李箱
aisle /ail/	n.	过道
video camera		摄像机
deplane /diːˈplein/	v.	下飞机

Exercises

1. Questions for discussion.

1）How will you greet the passengers when you are standing at the boarding gate?

2）How do you introduce yourself to the passengers when you first meet them on board?

3）What can you do for him if an old man can't find his seat?

4）What will you do if a passenger's seat is occupied by someone else?

5）What will you do if the passenger doesn't like sitting next to the emergency exit?

2. Oral practice.

Work with a partner to make up the following dialogues. Situational settings are as follows.

1）A man who is sitting in economy class wants to move to the first class or business class as he thinks it's too noisy and crowed here. A flight attendant comes up to help him.

2）A passenger standing in the aisle looks puzzled because he doesn't know how to put his big bag. At this time a flight attendant comes up.

Section B   Announcements

Boarding Announcement

Good morning (afternoon/evening), Ladies and Gentlemen,

Welcome aboard _____ Airlines from _____ to _____ (via _____). As you enter the cabin, please take your seat as soon as possible. Your seat number is indicated on the edge of the overhead bin. Please find your assigned seats, put your carry-on baggage in the overhead bin or under the seat in front of you. Please ask your flight attendant for help if you meet with some difficulties. We are glad to help you. Have a pleasant journey.

Thank you for your cooperation!

Re-checking boarding pass/card Announcement

Good morning (afternoon/evening), Ladies and Gentlemen：

Welcome aboard _____ Airlines. We will extend our warm welcome to every passenger. Would you please check your ticket and boarding card again to make sure you're boarding the right flight?

Thank you!

Prior to Take-off Announcement

Good morning, Ladies and Gentlemen,

May I have your attention please! The cabin door is now closed. We will take off shortly. For your safety, please be seated, fasten your seat belt, stow your tray table, return your footrest to its initial position and adjust your seat back to the upright position. Please don't use your mobile phones or certain electronic devices on board at any time. Laptop computers may not be used during take-off and landing. Please ensure that your mobile phone is turned off. Please be reminded that this is a non-smoking flight, so smoking is not allowed during the whole flight.

If you need assistance, please don't hesitate to ask a flight attendant. We wish you a pleasant journey.

Thank you!

Words and Expressions

indicate /ˈindikeit/	v.	指示,标明
overhead bin		舱顶行李架
carry-on baggage		手提行李
cooperation /kəuˌɔpəˈreiʃən/	n.	合作,配合

altitude /ˈæltitjuːd/		*n.*	高度,海拔
seat belt			安全带
stow /stəʊ/		*v.*	收起
footrest		*n.*	搁脚板
initial /iˈniʃəl/		*a.*	最初的,初始的
upright /ˈʌprait/		*a.*	直立的,垂直的
electronic /ilekˈtrɔnik/		*a.*	电子的
device /diˈvais/		*n.*	设备
laptop /ˈlæpˌtɔp/		*n.*	笔记本电脑
remind /riˈmaind/		*v.*	提醒
allow /əˈlaʊ/		*v.*	允许
hesitate /ˈheziteit/		*v.*	犹豫

Exercises

1. Match the English phrases in column A with the Chinese translations in column B.

A	B
(　　) a. Air China (CA)	1) 机舱门
(　　) b. British Airways (BA)	2) 登机牌
(　　) c. Hong Kong Airlines (HX)	3) 大陆航空公司(美国)
(　　) d. China Airlines (CI)	4) 电子设备
(　　) e. Continental Airlines (CO)	5) 英国航空公司
(　　) f. cabin door	6) 舱顶行李架
(　　) g. boarding card	7) 中国国际航空公司
(　　) h. seat belt	8) 香港航空有限公司
(　　) i. electronic devices	9) 中华航空公司(中国台湾)
(　　) j. overhead bin	10) 安全带

2. Translate the following sentences into English.

1) 您的座位号是多少呢? 我能看看您的登机牌吗?

2) 恐怕那位先生坐错座位了。请在这里稍等片刻。

3) 先生,您好。我能为您做点什么吗? 我看见您呼叫钮亮了。

4) 女士,您好。您可以将您的孩子抱在安全带的外面吗? 那样您的孩子会舒服些。

5) 不能把行李放在这里,因为过道不能堵塞。

6) 我第一次坐飞机,心里很紧张。

7) 女士,您好。我叫玛丽。我负责头等舱,如果您有什么需求请与我联系。

8) 我们所有机组人员很高兴能为您服务。

9) 请将您的手提行李放在头顶上方的行李柜内或是您前面的座位底下。

10) 您看到那边紧急出口旁靠过道的座位了吗?

3. Translate the following sentences into Chinese.

1) Excuse me, Miss, the girl over there is my girlfriend. She is feeling dizzy and nausea now. I wonder if I could sit next to her.

2) You should be seated in the assigned seat so as to ensure proper weight and balance for the plane when it takes off.

3) I don't know where to put my handbag. The overhead locker is full and I've tried to put it under the seat, yet it doesn't fit. Could you give me a hand?

4) Let me see, your seat number is 20A, in the middle of the cabin. Do you see the window seat next to the exit over there?

5) Would you mind assisting me to adjust the airflow? It's blowing right on my head. I feel a bit cold.

6) The seat number is indicated on the edge of each overhead compartment.

7) The old man follows a flight attendant to his seat, but the seat is occupied by a girl.

8) May I possibly upgrade to the business class? It's too noisy here in the economy class.

9) The boy over there is my friend. I wonder if I could sit next to him.

10) Excuse me, Sir. May I take another vacant seat? The place is so cramped that I can't stretch my leg.

4. Suppose you are a flight attendant. Now you are showing an old man to his seat and help him arrange his baggage. Please fill in the blanks of the following dialogue.

FA: Good afternoon, Sir. Welcome aboard.

P: Good afternoon! Where is my seat?

FA: (1) _____ .

P: Thank you. Where can I put my suitcase?

FA: (2) _____ .

P: Ok, could you help me?

FA: (3) _____ .

P: Miss, the temperature on board is too low. I feel a little cold.

FA: (4) _____ .

P: I'm extremely grateful to you.

FA: (5) _____ .

5. Fill in the blanks in the following sentences with the words given below. Change the form where necessary.

hesitate	identification	deplane	crease	allow
altitude	cooperation	purser	valuable	dizzy

1) After another glass of wine I start to feel _____ .

2) They had _____ closely in the planning of the project.

3) Would you mind packing the clothes carefully for me as I won't have them

_____ .

4) Please keep your _____ under your care in case of being stolen.

5) All passengers were _____ in five minutes after the emergency landing.

6) He _____ his baggage quickly among hundreds of others in the baggage

carousel.

7) The _____ is always ready to help passengers during a flight.

8) They don't _____ their children to go to the park themselves.

9) She didn't _____ for a moment about taking the job.

10) Our plane is flying at an _____ of 9 000 metres.

6. Complete the paragraph with the correct word in the box.

| distance   take   journey   remind   electronic |
| altitude   assistance   ensure   fasten   compartment |

Ladies and Gentlemen,

Good morning! Welcome aboard China Southern Airlines (CZ) Flight CZ350 to New York. The flying 1) _____ between Beijing and New York is about 10 kilometers. Our flight will 2)_____ 9 hours and 45 minutes. We will be flying at an 3)_____ of 8 500 meters.

We will take off shortly. Please be seated, 4)_____ your seat belt, and make sure your seat back and folding trays are in their full upright position. Meanwhile, your 5)_____ devices should be turned off. We will notify you when it is safe to use such devices. Please 6)_____ all your belongings is in the overhead 7)_____ or under the seat in front of you. We 8)_____ you that this is a non-smoking flight, so smoking is not allowed during the whole flight.

If you need 9)_____, please don't hesitate to ask a flight attendant. The chief purser Ella with all her crew members will be sincerely at your service. We wish you a pleasant 10)_____ .

Thank you!

Section C   Supplementary Reading

Paris Airport—Passengers with Reduced Mobility

Notify us as soon as you reach the airport by contacting our assistance service. You may do so outside or inside the terminal. An escort will be with you a few minutes after your all.

Reception outside the terminal

Whatever your transport is, once you reach the airport there are customer assistance terminals allowing you to notify us of your arrival.

Once you have called, an escort will join you by the customer assistance terminal to escort you through the terminal and up to the aircraft.

Using the customer assistance terminal

Just press the call button and you will be connected by audio and video link to our reception and assistance service. An escort will soon come to collect you.

The customer assistance terminal is fitted with an induction loop for the hearing-impaired. It is triggered in the same way as urban traffic lights with audio signals. You are picked up by car or taxi in front of the terminal. Ask your taxi or car driver to drop you off in one of the disabled areas of the drop-off point. The customer assistance terminals are located right next to these areas.

Location of drop-off points and customer assistance terminals.

Paris-Charles de Gaulle

- Terminal 1 - level depart - gate 6
- Terminal 2A - level depart - gate 5
- Terminal 2C - level depart - gate 12
- Terminal 2D - level depart - gate 6
- Terminal 2E - level depart - gate 7-8
- Terminal 2F - level depart - gate 10
- Terminal 2G - Departures hall
- Terminal 3 - Departures hall

Paris-Orly

- Terminal Sud: gate B
- Terminal Ouest: level Departures - gate C and Arrivals level arrivals - gate D

Leaving your car in the parking lot

In the parking lot near the terminals, slots have been reserved on each level for disabled or mobility-impaired passengers. You can notify your arrival via the customer assistance terminals nearby.

Arriving by public transport

At Paris-Charles de Gaulle

There is a customer assistance terminal:

- at the exit of the RER B "Charles de Gaulle 1" station. Access to terminals 1 and 3.
- at the exit of the RER B "Charles de Gaulle 2-TGV" station. Access to terminal 2.

At Paris-Orly

- West terminal: Orly bus stop (from Paris) and Arrival level, Gate D.
- South terminal: at the exit of the Orly shuttle train, just before the elevators and Gate C.

Reception inside the terminal

You may notify us of your arrival at the Paris Aéroport reception areas or check-in counters of your airline.

Reception area

Every terminal has at least one reception area with a reserved waiting room where our aid service personnel will come to collect you.

These areas have been specially equipped for your comfort.

Low counters for wheelchair-bound passengers.

Sound-proofed lounge with dimmer-equipped lights.

Location of the reception areas

At Paris-Charles de Gaulle
- Terminal 1: Level Departures - gate 02
- Terminal 2A: Level Departures between gates A5 et A6
- Terminal 2C: Level Departures between gates C5 et C6
- Terminal 2D: Level Departures between gates D6 et D7
- Terminal 2E: Level Departures between gates 7-8
- Terminal 2F: Level Departures between gates 8 et 10
- Terminal 2G: at the entrance of the terminal
- Terminal 3: at the entrance of the terminal

At Paris-Orly
- Terminal Ouest: Level Departure - between Hall 1 and 2, in front of Orlyval shuttle
- Terminal Sud: Level Departure - Gate B

Check-in counter of your airline

Notify your arrival to the airline personnel. They will inform our reception and assistance service center.

Connecting flight at the same airport

Our assistance service personnel will collect you on leaving your first flight and will escort you until you are seated in the next flight.

Connecting flight at another airport

Our assistance service personnel will collect you on leaving your first flight and will escort you to the transport of your choice (taxi, public transport etc.) to take you to the airport for your connecting flight.

When choosing the time of connecting flights, remember to notify your airline or travel agent of the time you will need to cover the distance between the various terminals.

Questions for discussion.

1. How do you use the customer assistance terminal?

2. What's the location of reception areas about Terminal 3?

3. What are reception areas equipped with?

4. Where is Terminal 2?

5. When choosing the time of connecting flights, what should you keep in mind?

Section D   Interview English

Daily hot topic:

Hometown

The typical questions on daily hot topic.

1. Where is your hometown?

2. Do you like your hometown? Why?

3. Is there anything special about the history of your hometown?

4. What specialities are there in your hometown?

5. What kinds of places of interest are there in your hometown?

The following question has been usually asked when you have an interview. There is an example. The answer is given for your reference.

Would you like to say something about your hometown?

My hometown is Shenyang. Shenyang is the capital city of Liaoning Province in Northeast of China. It has a long history and is a heavy industrial center of China. Now there is a great change. The streets have become wider, many shabby houses have been torn down and many new mansions have been built. People are very kind, honest and friendly to the strangers. In general, I love my hometown.

Role-play practice:

You want to be a flight attendant and have an interview. The interviewer asks you to introduce your hometown to them. Please make an interview role-play with your partner.

Unit 3

Safety Check before Take-off

Lead-in questions

1. What would you say to a passenger who is using his computer/mobile phone when the aircraft is taking off?
2. How do you advise all the passengers to keep their seat belts securely fastened during the whole flight?
3. Do you know some basic knowledge to protect yourself from the effects of severe turbulence?

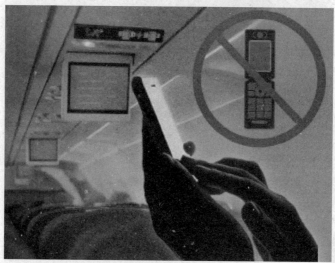

Section A Dialogues

Dialogue one

Setting：A flight attendant named Linda comes around to do the pre-flight safety check. She finds that an old man is smoking in his seat. Thus she comes up to him.

(P＝passenger)

Linda：Excuse me, Sir. Please put out your cigarette now. Smoking is not permitted here.

P：Sorry, is there any smoking section on board? I'm not feeling quite well myself, so I want to smoke in order to relax myself.

Linda：I'm sorry to hear that! This is a non-smoking flight. Are you sick?

P：No, I feel very nervous whenever taking a plane, especially pre-flight.

Linda：I'd like to tell you some ways to relieve your stress and improve your mood. Please close your eyes, remain calm and breathe deeply. You will feel better after a while.

P：I see, let me try. Thank you for your help.

Linda：It's my pleasure. By the way, why don't you fasten your seat belt?

P：Er...I fastened it just now but it was too tight, which made me more uncomfortable. Thus I loosened it. Must I keep it fastened?

Linda：Yes, for your safety, your seat belt has to be fastened during the take-off, landing and flying while the seat belt sign is on. By the way, the seat belt can be adjusted if you feel too tight.

P：Oh? I don't know how to adjust it. Would you like to help me?

Linda：Of course, Just slip the belt into the buckle and pull the belt. Look! This side can be adjusted. Is it Ok now?

P：Yes, it's really very nice of you. Er...now I feel much better while talking with you! Why?

Linda：Because you divert your attention as chatting with me. It's also a way to relieve your nervousness.

P：Oho! Thanks a lot.

Linda：Don't mention it. Please, press the call button if you have any other problems.

P：I don't know how to express my appreciation.

Linda：It's our duty to serve you well.

Dialogue two

Setting：The plane is taking off soon. A flight attendant named Cathy is walking around in the cabin. She notices that a young girl is using her laptop, then she comes up to her.

Cathy：Excuse me, Miss. Would you please stop using your laptop and switch it off?

P：Why? I'm surfing the Internet.

Cathy：You aren't permitted to use your laptop during taking off or landing because it might interfere with the navigation system.

P：When can I use it?

Cathy：You may use it when the aircraft reaches its cruising altitude.

P：Ok，yet I hope you would remind me about it.

Cathy：Sure. By the way，you should return your seat back to the upright position.

P：Er...but I don't know how to return it.

Cathy：Just press the button on your armrest.

P：Oh！I see. Like this？It's all right now.

Cathy：Good job！

P：May I go to the washroom now？

Cathy：Sorry，Miss. The plane is taking off. You must keep seated with your seat belt fastened. It means you can't move until the plane enters its cruising altitude.

P：Will it take a long time？

Cathy：Not a long time.

P：All right. How long will it take to fly from Beijing to Guangzhou？

Cathy：Flying time will be 2 hours and 30 minutes.

P：Where will we pass over？

Cathy：On this air route we will be passing over the Provinces of Hebei，Henan，Hubei，Hunan，Guangdong. And we will cross the Yellow River，and the Yangtze River.

P：What's the speed of our aircraft？

Cathy：The cruising speed will be about _____ kilometers per hour. What else do you want to ask？

P：No，thanks.

Cathy：If that so. I'll go and have a safety check in the cabin as the aircraft is about to take off.

P：Ok.

Words and Expressions

severe /si'viə/	*a.*	十分严重的
turbulence /'tɜːbjələns/	*n.*	紊流，强气流
cigarette /ˌsigə'ret/	*n.*	香烟
permit /pə'mit /	*v.*	允许
relieve /ri'liːv/	*v.*	缓解
loosen /'luːsən/	*v.*	解开
adjust /ə'dʒʌst/	*v.*	调整
buckle /'bʌkl/	*n.*	搭扣
divert /dai'vəːt/	*v.*	转移（某人）的注意力
call button		呼叫按钮

surf the internet		上网
interfere /ˌintəˈfiə/	*n.*	干涉
navigation /ˌnæviˈgeiʃən/	*n.*	航行
cruising /ˈkruːziŋ/	*a.*	巡航的
washroom /ˈwɔʃˌruːm/	*n.*	洗手间
province /ˈprɔvins/	*n.*	省份

Exercises

1. Questions for discussion.

1) How do you do if a passenger uses her mobile phone before take-off?

2) What should you say when you have a safety check?

3) When can the passengers use their mobile phone, laptop or ipad?

4) Why can't the passengers use their mobile phones during the whole flight?

5) The aircraft is going to take off. Yet a little girl wants to go to the lavatory. What should you do?

2. Oral practice.

Work with a partner to make up the following dialogues. Situational settings are as follows.

1) It is the first time for an old woman to take a plane. She doesn't know how to fasten her seat belt and adjust her seat. Her face is rather pale. At this time, a flight attendant comes to the passenger to help her.

2) The plane is taking off shortly. You notice a man using his laptop with a lighted cigarette dangling from his mouth. A flight attendant comes up to him, meanwhile, his mobile phone rings suddenly.

Section B   Announcements

Safety Demonstration Video

Ladies and gentlemen,

Thank you for taking flight _____ . Now we'll be showing a brief safety demonstration video. This information can help you if there is an emergency situation, so it is important to pay close attention. If you have any questions, please contact the flight attendants.

Safety Demonstration by the Flight Attendant

Ladies and Gentlemen,

We will now explain the use of the life vest, oxygen mask, seat belt and location of the exit.

Your life vest is located under your seat. To put the vest on, slip it over your head, fasten the buckles and pull the straps tight around your waist. Then, pull the inflation tab down firmly, but don't inflate it in the cabin. If your vest needs further inflation, blow into the tubes on either side of your vest.

Your oxygen mask is in a compartment above your head, and will drop automatically if oxygen is needed. When it drops, pull the mask firmly toward you to start the flow of oxygen. Place the mask over your nose and mouth and slip the elastic band over your head. Within a few seconds, the oxygen flow will begin.

In the interest of your safety, there are two belts on the sides of your seat that can be buckled together around your waist. Please keep them fastened while the aircraft is taxiing, taking off, in turbulence and landing. To release, lift up on the top plate of the buckle.

There are eight emergency exits on this aircraft. They are located in the front, the rear and the middle section. Please follow the emergency lights which are on the floor and exits to evacuate in the event of emergency. For further information you will find safety instruction card in the seat pocket in front of you.

Thank you.

Announcement for introduction of cabin crew after take-off

Ladies and gentlemen：

I am _____, your chief purser. On behalf of _____ airlines, we extend the most sincere greetings to you. Let me introduce my cabin crew to you. This is _____. This is _____ and this is _____. We'll do our utmost to provide you good service and hope you a pleasant trip. Thank you!

Words and Expressions

demonstration /demən'streiʃ(ə)n/	n.	演示，示范
contact /'kɔntækt/	v.	联系
life vest /jacket		救生衣
location /lə(ʊ)'keiʃ(ə)n/	n.	位置
strap /stræp/	n.	带子
waist /weist/	n.	腰
inflate /in'fleit/	v.	使充气，(使)膨胀
tube /tju:b/	n.	管子
automatically /ˌɔːtə'mætikəli/	ad.	自动地
extinguish /ik'stiŋwiʃ/	v.	熄灭
elastic band /i'læstik//bænd/	n.	弹力带
taxi /'tæksi/	v.	滑行

release /riˈliːs/	v.	解开,松开
rear /riə/	n.	后部
evacuation /iˌvækjʊˈeiʃ(ə)n/	n.	撤离
safety instructions		安全说明
extend /ɪkˈstend/	v.	给予,表达
sincere /sinˈsiə/	a.	真诚的
crew /kruː/	n.	全体机务人员
utmost /ˈʌtməust/	a.	极度的,最大的

Exercises

1. Match the English phrases in column A with the Chinese translations in column B.

A	B
(　　) a. Air Europe（AE）	1）中国南方航空公司
(　　) b. safety instructions	2）导航系统
(　　) c. Cathay Pacific Airways（CX）	3）德国汉莎航空公司
(　　) d. China Southern Airline（CZ）	4）安全带指示灯
(　　) e. electronic device	5）东方航空公司（美国）
(　　) f. navigation system	6）安全说明
(　　) g. Eastern Airlines（EA）	7）欧洲航空公司（英国）
(　　) h. safety demonstration	8）电子设备
(　　) i. seat belt sign	9）安全演示
(　　) j. Lufthansa German Airline（LH）	10）国泰航空公司（中国香港）

2. Translate the following sentences into English.

1）当安全带指示灯亮着时,请系好您的安全带。

2）此架飞机上有几个安全出口,如果需要紧急撤离,请找离您最近的安全出口。

3）请恢复您的座位及脚踏板到原始位置。

4）靠窗边的旅客请您协助我们将遮光板拉开。

5）为了确保飞行和通信系统的正常操作,请您关闭所有的电子设备。

6）请系好安全带,特别是在飞机滑行、起飞和降落的时候。

7）请您立即将烟熄灭,飞机上全程都不允许吸烟。

8）我们现在向您展示救生衣、安全带及氧气面罩的使用方法。

9）飞机正在着陆,离开座位很危险。所以请系好安全带。

10）想要了解更详细的信息,请参考你前面座椅口袋里的安全须知卡。

3. Translate the following sentences into Chinese.

1）Please make sure that your seat belt is fastened, your seat is upright, and your tray table is closed.

2）Would you please return your seat back to the upright position? Just press the button on your armrest.

3) Please ensure all your baggage is in the overhead compartments or under the seat in front of you.

4) The use of the lavatory will be suspended during take-off and landing.

5) In accordance with regulations, to ensure a clean and comfortable cabin environment, smoking is not allowed during the flight.

6) Oxygen masks will drop automatically from a compartment above your head if oxygen is needed in the cabin.

7) The lights located on the floor will guide you to the exits if an emergency arises.

8) Could you tell me how to fasten the seat belt?

9) Our plane will take off at once, please be seated, fasten your seat belt, and ensure your seat back is straight up.

10) Your life jacket is in the compartment under your seat / over your head.

4. Suppose you are a flight attendant. Now you are serving an unaccompanied child in the cabin. She doesn't fasten her seat belt. Please fill in the blanks of the following dialogue.

FA: Excuse me, Helen. Would you please fasten your seat belt?

Child: Oh, must I fasten my seat belt? It makes me feel uncomfortable if I wear it.

FA: Of course. For your safety, you'd better fasten it.

Child: But I don't know how to fasten it. (1) _____.

FA: Just slip the belt into the buckle and pull tight. Is it OK?

Child: (2) _____.

Must I fasten the seat belt at all times?

FA: Er... (3) _____.

Child: Yeah, when will we arrive at Beijing International Airport?

FA: (4) _____.

Child: (5) _____.

5. Fill in the blanks in the following sentences with the words given below. Change the form where necessary.

> adjust   automatically   ditch   securely   turbulence
> relieve   interfere   inflate   divert   loosen

1) I wish my parents would stop _____ and let me make my own decisions.

2) The tables on board were _____ firmly to the floor.

3) The war _____ people's attention away from the economic crisis.

4) Please try to hold the back of the seat in front of you and place your head between your arm, because we are preparing for emergency _____.

5) Being able to tell the truth at last seemed to _____ her.

6) You should _____ your language to the age of your passenger while serving on board.

7) The severe _____ caused the plane to turn over.

8) The boy _____ the screw with the help of his father.

9) The life vest must not be _____ inside the aircraft, as this will inhibit the exit of passengers in an emergency.

10) The oxygen mask will _____ drop down above each passenger's head in the event of loss of cabin pressure.

6. Complete the paragraph with the correct word in the box.

ditches introduce emergency belt signs
inflate blow information appear necessary

Ladies and Gentlemen.

May we have your attention, please? We will 1)_____ the use of seat belt, life jacket and oxygen mask.

There are two pieces of 2)_____ on your seat. You need insert one side into the buckle and adjust it as 3)_____ . Please keep your seat belt securely fastened while the fasten seat belt 4)_____ are on.

You should put on the life jacket once the plane 5)_____ . Firstly, slip it over your head. Then fasten the buckles and the straps tightly around your waist.

Finally 6)_____ the life jacket by pulling the inflation tabs. If the life jacket isn't inflated enough, you can use mouth tubes to 7)_____ .

Your oxygen mask will 8)_____ in front of you automatically in the event of 9)_____ on board. Place the mask over your nose and mouth and slip the elastic band over your head, then the oxygen will flow out.

For further 10)_____ , please refer to safety leaflet in the seat pocket in front of you. Thank you.

Section C   Supplementary Reading

Pre-flight Safety Demonstration

The pre-flight safety briefing (also known as a pre-flight demonstration, in-flight safety briefing, in-flight safety demonstration, safety instructions, or simply the safety video) is a detailed explanation given before take-off to airline passengers about the safety features of the aircraft they are aboard.

Aviation regulations do not state how an airline should deliver the briefing, only that "The operator of an aircraft shall ensure that all passengers are orally briefed before each take-off". As a result, depending on the in-flight entertainment system in the aircraft, as well as the airline's policy, airlines may deliver a pre-recorded briefing or provide a live demonstration. A live demonstration is performed by a flight attendant/s standing up in the aisles, while another flight attendant narrates over the public address system. A pre-recorded briefing may feature audio only, or may take the form of a video (audio plus visual). Pre-flight safety briefings typically last two to six minutes. In consideration for travelers don't speaking the airline's official language and for the passengers with hearing problems, the video may feature subtitles, or may be repeated in another language.

Some safety videos are made by using three-dimensional graphics. Other videos are humorous stories, celebrities, or popular movies. Many safety videos are uploaded to YouTube. Cebu Pacific choreographed the entire demonstration to Lady Gaga's "Just Dance" and Katy Perry's "California Gurls" as an experiment during one of their flights. The flight attendant in the latest Delta Air Lines video has become an internet celebrity known as Deltalina.

Flight attendants are trained to calmly instruct passengers how to respond, given the type of emergency. Research conducted at the University of New South Wales Australia questions the effectiveness of these briefings in conveying key safety messages for passengers to recall and act upon in an emergency. In one study, a range of pre-recorded safety briefings were tested. One safety briefing contained humor, the other was void of humor (said to reflect a standard briefing), and another used a celebrity to tell the importance of the safety briefing and the messages. Not long after being exposed to the briefing, individuals recalled approximately 50% of the key safety messages from the briefing featuring the celebrity, 45% from the briefing containing humor, and 32% from the briefing void of both a celebrity and humor. Two hours post exposure to the pre-flight safety briefings, recall decreased on average by 4% from the original levels across all conditions.

Required elements

Airlines are required to orally brief their passengers before each take-off. This requirement is set by their nations' civil aviation authority, under the recommendation of the International Civil Aviation Organization. How they do this is up to the airline, but most (if not all) elect to do this through a safety briefing or demonstration delivered to all passengers at the same time. A safety demonstration typically covers all these aspects, not necessarily in this order:

Demonstrating to passengers means telling passengers that the safety card shows the brace position and must be adopted on hearing the "Brace" command during an emergency landing. (sometimes called the safety position, but not required in the United States and certain other countries)

The use of the seat belt.

Some airlines recommend or require that passengers keep their seat belt fastened all the time in case of unexpected turbulence.

The requirement

Passengers must comply with lighted signs, posted cards, and crew members instructions (Generally only included in safety demonstrations on Australian, New Zealand, and American carriers whereas the CASA (AU), CAA (NZ)and FAA (US)require it to be stated). Most other airlines only include the seat belt and no smoking signs.

The location and use of the emergency exits, evacuation slides and emergency floor lighting.

All passengers should locate their nearest exit, which may be behind them. The requirement for passengers sitting in an emergency exit row (varies by country and airline) is that in the United States, exit row passengers may be required to assist the crew in an evacuation. and that all passengers must leave all carry-on bags behind during an evacuation.

The use of the oxygen mask (not included on some turboprops which do not fly high enough to need supplemental oxygen in a decompression emergency) with associated reminders:

That the passenger should always fit his or her own mask on before helping children, the disabled, or persons requiring assistance. That even though oxygen will be flowing to the mask, the plastic bag may not inflate (required in the United States after a woman fatally removed her mask thinking it was not working). Some planes such as the Boeing 787 do not include plastic bags in the oxygen masks.

The location and use of the life vests, life rafts and flotation devices (not always included if the flight does not overfly or fly near vast masses of water although is required by the FAA (US)on any aircraft equipped with life vests)

The use of passenger seat cushions as flotation devices. (typically only included on aircraft that do not provide life vests)

That smoking is not allowed on board, including in the lavatories. (some airlines, including the US on all Domestic flights and international flights going to and from the US, also ban electronic cigarettes)

That US federal law prohibits tampering with, disabling or destroying lavatory smoke detectors.

That the use of mobile phones is not allowed during flight, unless placed in "airplane mode" or the wireless capability is turned off.

That laptops and other electronics may only be used once the aircraft is at cruising altitude and the Captain turns off the fasten seat-belt sign.

That passengers must ask a flight attendant prior to using electronics.

That seatbacks and tray tables should be in their upright and locked position, headrest stowed, and carry-on luggage stowed in the overhead locker or underneath a seat prior to takeoff.

To review the safety information card prior to takeoff or to follow along during the demonstration.

Questions for discussion.

1. What is the pre-flight safety briefing?

2. What does the operator of an aircraft make sure of?

3. How long do pre-flight safety briefings usually last?

4. How many aspects does a safety demonstration typically cover?

5. What do passengers do before helping those who need help?

Section D   Interview English

Daily hot topics:

Your hobbies

The typical questions on daily hot topics.

1. What's your hobby/interest?

2. Did you take part in any extra activities when you studied at school?

3. What do you usually do in your spare time?

4. Can you tell us an interest that you particularly enjoy?

5. How do you think of your character?

The following question has been usually asked when you have an interview. There is an example. The answer is given for your reference.

Would you introduce your character or hobbies to us?

I'm an honest, responsible and courteous person. I think I'm very outgoing by nature. I like being with people and always enjoy helping others. I was quite active in the university and also was a member of the Student Union and organized some activities. In my spare time, I like reading, listening to music and traveling. Reading makes me think positively. Traveling broadens my horizon and enriches my knowledge. I'm good at playing the violin. I wish I could be a member of your airlines; thus, I will have the chance to play the violin for you.

Role-play practice:

You want to be a flight attendant and have an interview. You are asked to say something about your interest. Please have an interview role-play with your partner.

Unit 4

Reasons for Delay

Lead-in questions

1. Have you ever met the situation that the aircraft was departure delayed when you took an aircraft?

2. Could you list some possible reasons for a delayed departure?

3. How do you make an apology to a passenger if the flight is delayed due to the bad weather condition?

Section A   Dialogues

Dialogue one

Setting: A passenger heard an announcement that his flight will be delayed, so he asks an airport crew for the reasons.

（AC: Airport crew   P: Passenger）

P：Excuse me，Miss. Just now I heard from the announcement that my flight CX2386 has been delayed.

AC：Yes，It has been delayed.

P：Why has it been delayed?

AC：The delay is due to some mechanical troubles. The engineers are making a careful examination of the aircraft.

P：Is it serious? When do you think we'll be able to take off?

AC：It's hard to say. But don't worry about it！ You shall be informed when the troubles are solved.

P：Ok. Thanks a lot.

(*Twenty minutes later*)

P：Hi，Miss！ It is now 25 minutes past the departure time，yet we haven't got any information.

AC：I apologize for having kept you waiting for some time. Just now we got the news that the mechanical troubles had been solved，but we have to wait for the plane ahead of us to take off.

P：How long are we going to wait?

AC：We haven't got an exact time for departure now. I think it won't take too long.

P：Oh，my God. It's really terrible.

AC：I am terribly sorry for the inconvenience brought to you.

P：I hope I never meet this situation again.

AC：Thank you for your cooperation.

Dialogue two

Setting：It is 8：00 a. m. ten minutes past the scheduled departure time，yet it has not taken off. A passenger presses the call button. Flight attendant Laura comes up to her.

Laura：Excuse me，Madam. Is there anything I can do for you?

P：May I ask you a question?

Laura：Yes，please.

P：Now it's 8：10 a. m. The ticket says it will take off at 8：00 a. m. It is already 10 minutes past the scheduled departure time. Why hasn't the flight taken off? Is there anything wrong with the flight?

Laura：Sorry，Madam. Based on the regulation of CAAC，the departure time on your ticket refers to the time for closing cabin doors，but not for taking off.

P：Oh，thank you. By the way，it's terribly hot. I can't stand the heat. Could you adjust the air conditioner cooler?

Laura：Ok. I will do it for you.

(15 minutes later, the flight still does not take off. The passenger asks the cabin attendant again.)

P：Hi，Miss. It's 8：25 a.m. now and another 15 minutes has passed. Why hasn't the flight taken off yet? Could you explain it?

Laura：I'm very sorry to tell you that we've got the latest information from Beijing International Airport that there is a heavy thunderstorm near Beijing Airport. Therefore, the flight has to be delayed for it. I really apologize for having kept you waiting for a long time.

P：Then how long will we wait?

Laura：We can't make sure the exact time for departure at present. Please wait for a moment. If there is any further information, we will inform you as soon as possible.

P：I hope it will not take too long, or I will be late for my connecting flight.

Laura：What's the departure time of your connecting flight?

P：The departure time is 11：40 a.m. If we arrive there on schedule, there are 55 minutes left.

Laura：Don't worry, Madam. If you miss the flight, go to the transit counter and they'll make a new arrangement for you.

P：I hope our flight will take off soon.

Laura：I hope so, too. I am very sorry for the delay and the inconvenience brought to you.

P：It doesn't matter. It isn't your fault.

Words and Expressions

delay /di'lei/	*n. /v.*	延时，耽搁
departure /di'pɑːtʃə/	*n.*	离开，出发
mechanical /mi'kænikəl/	*a.*	机械的
inconvenience /ˌinkən'viːnjəns/	*n.*	不方便
schedule /'ʃedjuːəl/	*v.*	排定，安排
CAAC(Civil Aviation Administration of China)		中国民航
air conditioner		空调设施
thunderstorm /'θʌndə'stɔːm/	*n.*	雷电交加的暴风雨
connecting flight		转接班机
transit counter		转机柜台
fault /fɔːlt/	*n.*	过错

Exercises

1. Questions for discussion.

1) The passengers are very angry because the aircraft has been delayed for two

hours. How will you comfort the passengers at this time?

2) Does the departure time on your ticket refer to the time for closing cabin doors or taking off based on the regulation of CAAC?

3) What should the passenger do if he can't catch his connecting flight?

4) The plane is delayed for an hour due to the air traffic control at the airport. How can you explain this situation to the passengers?

5) How will you answer a passenger if she asks you the reasons of the delayed departure which you have no idea of?

2. Oral Practice.

Work with a partner to make up dialogues. Situational settings are as follows.

1) The plane is delayed because of the air traffic control. You need explain the situation to the passengers.

2) The plane is delayed due to the late arrival of joining passengers. You need explain the situation to the passengers.

Section B　Announcements

Brief Delay Departure Announcement

Ladies and Gentlemen,

May I have your attention please! I am _____, your (chief) purser. On behalf of _____ Airlines, we extend the most sincere greetings to you. We are sorry for the brief delay due to _____ (aircraft late arrival/air traffic control/ unfavorable weather conditions/ mechanical problems/ cargo loading/ airport congestion/waiting for some passengers).

Our team is looking forward to making your journey with us, a safe and pleasant one.

Thank you for your understanding.

Delayed Departure Announcement

Ladies and Gentlemen,

I am _____, your (chief) purser. We sincerely apologize for the delay due to _____ (aircraft late arrival/air traffic control/ unfavorable weather conditions/ mechanical problems/ cargo loading/ airport congestion/waiting for some passengers).

Together with my team, we will do our utmost to make the rest of your journey as pleasant and comfortable as possible. We thank you for your patience and cooperation.

Comfort Passengers Announcement

Ladies and Gentlemen,

This is your (chief) purser speaking. We are terribly sorry for the delay of our flight due to _____ . Because your safety is our primary concern, safety first is our guideline. Thank you for your kind understanding, patience and cooperation.

Problems Solved Announcement

Ladies and Gentlemen：

We are very happy to inform you that we have received take-off clearance from CAAC. Our plane will depart in ten minutes. Please confirm that your seat belt is securely fastened, your mobile phone and all electronic devices are switched off. We sincerely apologize for the delay in departure and appreciate your understanding.

Words and Expressions

air traffic control		空中交通管制
unfavorable /ʌnˈfeivərəbəl/	*a.*	不利的
mechanical /miˈkænik(ə)l/	*a.*	机械的
cargo /ˈkɑːgəʊ/	*n.*	（船、飞机、车辆等运载的）货物
congestion /kənˈdʒestʃən/	*n.*	拥挤，阻塞
patience /ˈpeiʃ(ə)ns/	*n.*	耐心
primary /ˈpraim(ə)ri/	*a.*	主要的，首要的
guideline /ˈgaidlain/	*n.*	指导方针
clearance /ˈkliərəns/	*n.*	许可，批准
confirm /kənˈfɜːm/	*v.*	确认
sincerely /sinˈsiəli/	*ad.*	真诚地
appreciate / əˈpriːʃieit/	*v.*	感激，感谢

Exercises

1. Match the English phrases in column A with the Chinese translations in column B.

A	B
(　　) a. American Airlines（AA）	1）技术故障
(　　) b. Air France（AF）	2）空中交通管制
(　　) c. Shandong Airlines(SC)	3）空调
(　　) d. Air Macau（NX）	4）延时起飞
(　　) e. Spring Air（9C）	5）起飞许可
(　　) f. take-off clearance	6）山东航空公司
(　　) g. air traffic control	7）澳门航空公司
(　　) h. delayed departure	8）美国航空公司
(　　) i. mechanical trouble	9）法国航空公司
(　　) j. air conditioner	10）春秋航空

2. Translate the following sentences into English.

1）我们很抱歉地告知您，由于飞机出现机械故障，您的航班将被取消。

2）打扰一下，请问前往纽约的 CA560 次航班多久才能起飞？

3）由于能见度低，机场关闭，我们不能起飞了。

4）我们须等待跑道上的冰被清除才能起飞。

5）一旦天气转好，飞机马上起飞。

6）由于地面有大雾，本次航班将延误 1 个小时。

7）如果有进一步消息，我们会马上通知您的。

8）恐怕我们得等机场的天气好转才能起飞。

9）由于机场跑道的拥堵，几架飞机都在等待起飞。

10）由于目的地机场恶劣的天气条件，CA5645 号航班被取消。

3. Translate the following sentences into Chinese.

1）We are terribly sorry for the inconvenience we have brought to you. I suggest you change a flight right now.

2）We'll have to stay here overnight because the flight MF5688 has been cancelled tonight. Please take your belongings and prepare to disembark.

3）Don't worry. We'll provide free accommodation for every passenger after a while.

4）Owing to the air traffic control, we'll wait until a take-off clearance is given.

5）We've got the latest information from Shenyang Taoxian International Airport that Flight 9C6580 has been delayed.

6）If the flight was missed you will have to stay for four hours at the airport and wait for the next flight.

7）We regret to announce that your arrival time will be postponed to half past six at night.

8）We have been informed that the boarding time will be delayed because of the mechanical troubles.

9）Excuse me, Sir. We have been waiting for taking off for more than one hour. What's wrong with the flight?

10）As the weather is so changeable, please listen to the latest announcement about your flight.

4. Suppose you are an airport crew. Now a plane is delayed at the airport for 40 minutes. You explain the situation to the passengers. Please fill in the blanks of the following dialogue.

P：Excuse me, Miss. I heard from the announcement just now that my flight has been delayed. What's the reason?

AC：(1)_____.

P：How long will we wait for?

AC：(2)_____.

P：Oh? But I have booked a connecting flight heading for Shanghai. I have to catch it.

AC:(3)_____. I suggest you change the flight right now.

P:But I don't know how to deal with the formalities.

AC:(4)_____.

P:It's very kind of you.

AC:(5)_____.

5. Fill in the blanks in the following sentences with the words given below. Change the form where necessary.

> overcome   clearance   button   delay   inconvenient
> schedule   mechanical   thunderstorm   departure   congestion

1) The new bridge has been finished one year ahead of _____ .

2) We are sorry to inform you that due to _____ reasons, your flight will be delayed until 16:30.

3) We have received no news of her since her _____ from the island .

4) He _____ injury to win the Olympic gold medal.

5) The pilot was waiting for _____ for take-off.

6) We have encountered heavy _____ and severe turbulence during the flight.

7) We are informed that the heavy fog causes the _____ of all flights here.

8) Many of the domestic airports are heavily _____ during the National Day.

9) Mary pressed the _____ and waited for the lift.

10) We apologize for the delay and regret any _____ it may have caused.

6. Complete the paragraph with the correct word in the box.

> congestion   belongings   information   inform   depart
> fairly   clearance   staff   lounge   runway

We are sorry to 1)_____ you that due to 2)_____ on the 3)_____ ,it will be a 4)_____ long time before we are able to 5)_____ . We have to wait for the take-off 6)_____ . Please take all your 7)_____ and follow our ground 8)_____ to the waiting 9)_____ in the terminal. Further 10)_____ will be given there.

Section C   Supplementary Reading

Nine Reasons of Flight Delays or Cancellations

In an ideal world, your travel scenario would go something like this: First show up at the airport, check in and get your boarding passes, then get through security, board your plane, and take off. If you're an occasional traveler, perhaps every one of your flights has followed this pattern. But what happens when it doesn't?

There are certain events entirely beyond your control which could impact your flight. When flight delays and cancellations occur at airports, they are usually due to one of the nine following reasons. Here's a look at why these events affect your flight, and what you should do if they happen to you.

Security

When standing at the back of a serpentine line weaving all over the security area, most travelers have one thought in their minds: *Will this cause me to miss my flight*? Certain events such as holidays can increase the number of people in the security line, but other times these backups can happen for seemingly no reason. While security staff often directs people over to shorter lines when their flights are about to depart, sometimes the airport is simply overwhelmed. It's a coin toss as to whether or not the airline will hold the flight for passengers stuck in security, which affects not only the travelers in line, but also the ones on the plane waiting to taxi to the runway.

Weather

Winter storms, lightning storms and strong winds will keep planes on the ground for the safety of everyone involved. It is always recommended that passengers check the status of their flights before heading to the airport, especially if you know that there is a storm on the way. Airlines can't be responsible for delays or cancellations due to inclement weather, but once the storms clear out they will often reschedule you onto the next available flight at no extra charge. In the case of extreme delays or mass cancellations, most airlines will typically offer refunds to their customers.

National Aviation System

The National Aviation System (NAS) is a broad term which encompasses many different factors that might impact flight timetable. This might include non-severe weather events, heavy air traffic, air traffic control delays, and airport operations. These reasons may sound vague, but they account for nearly 25% of all airport delays or cancellations. If your flight is affected just due to general airport conditions, you may have some recourse.

Late Arriving Aircraft

Planes are put into heavy rotation. Usually, the plane that took passengers from Chicago to LA will be refueled, checked, and turned around a few hours later to take passengers on the return route. Of course, if a flight is significantly delayed longer, it can end up affecting passengers at other airports who were scheduled to take the same aircraft to their destination. This is how a blizzard in Boston can wind up causing travel headaches in Dallas. Passengers who missed their connections should be compensated by the airline, and switched to new flights.

Fueling

It can take up to 2 hours to refuel a jet, especially the large craft. If there are issues getting your plane properly fueled in a timely manner, this could cause a significant delay. The issue with this type of delay is that you often won't know about it until you get to the airport. If something like this happens, it is important to know your rights as a traveler.

Congestion in Air Traffic

Over 80 000 flights cross the US every day. That may seem like a huge number, but air traffic control towers are equipped to handle it all. Issues begin to arise when air traffic is particularly heavy due to a holiday or other events, and flights may be delayed. If you know you are traveling on a particularly busy day, be sure to check your flight status several times leading up to your departure for the airport.

Maintenance Issues

If it is discovered that there is a maintenance issue with your aircraft, the flight will not embark until the issue has been fully addressed. Sometimes, these issues are being worked on even as passengers board the plane, meaning the delay you experience might take place entirely on the tarmac. Other times, in the case of larger issues, your airline might make the call to switch planes entirely for the safety of everyone involved.

Baggage Loading

Long lines at check-in might mean that there is baggage being loaded onto your plane right up until the last possible minute. These delays are aggravating, but ideally, they are meant to ensure that everyone's luggage makes it to their destination with them. If you've ever made it to your destination with your carry on and nothing else, then you already know this isn't always the case.

Computer Glitches

Even a relatively small computer hiccup can cause massive delays and cancellations all across the globe. You may have read about the recent outages with companies like Delta or United Continental, each of which affected thousands of passengers in all different locations. No matter where you are traveling to or from, if your flight is affected by a computer issue on the airlines' end, you should be compensated. Travelers should have the option of getting a refund, or changing flights.

Many passengers feel a lot of anxiety about their flights, and that's completely understandable. Thousands of people are trying to make connecting flights, reach family and friends, or attend important meetings every single day. A cancellation or delay could have a huge negative impact on their travel.

Questions for discussion.

1. What are the nine reasons of flight delays or cancellations? Illustrate one of them.

2. Will airlines take responsibility for the delay due to bad weather? If not, what will they do?

3. Talk about one of your experiences due to flight delay.

4. What is understandable due to cancellation or delay?

5. What should you make sure if you are travelling on a busy day?

Section D　Interview English

Daily hot topic:

Career

The typical questions on daily hot topic.

1. What are your career goals?

2. What interests you most about being a flight attendant?

3. Why do you want to be a flight attendant?

4. What kind of work experience do you have?

5. Do you think what kind of employee you will be?

The following question has been usually asked when you have an interview. There is an example. The answer is given for your reference.

Why do you want to be a steward or a stewardess and what is the most important thing about being a steward or a stewardess?

Firstly, I like this job. Then, I think my character is suitable for working as a flight attendant. I'm a friendly, responsible and hard-working girl. I've always enjoyed helping others and working with others. I'm easy-going and open-minded; I can accept new things easily. Next, I like traveling very much. If I work as a flight attendant, I will have more chances to visit some interesting places all over the world.

The most important thing of being a flight attendant is to ensure the safety of all passengers and make them feel comfortable and relaxed during the flight. To be honest, flying is a stressful thing. If a flight attendant can ease that tension it will make a favorable impression for the airline.

Role-play practice：

You want to be a flight attendant and have an interview. You are asked what special qualities a flight attendant should have. Please have an interview role-play with your partner.

Unit 5
Drink and Meal Service

Lead-in questions

1. Can you speak out some alcoholic and non-alcoholic drinks served on board?

2. What are the procedures of western meal?

3. How do you explain to a passenger who has asked for a cup of coffee for quite a long time?

Section A   Dialogues

Dialogue one

Setting: A passenger is pressing the call button so the flight attendant named Lucie comes up to him.

(P: passenger)

Lucie: Is there anything I can do for you, Sir?

P1: Now it's too hot sitting in the cabin. I feel very hot. Why don't you make the air-conditioner cooler?

Lucie: I'm sorry to hear that. I will inform our captain to adjust the air-conditioner, then you will feel better.

P1: I'm also very thirsty. Why don't you serve some drinks for us?

Lucie: We will offer you drinks shortly. We are preparing for them.

P1: Please quickly.

Lucie: OK. Please wait a moment.

(*Lucie comes up to him again with the cart*)

Lucie: Excuse me, Sir. What would you like to drink?

P1:I have no idea. I only want to have cold drinks.

Lucie:Er...how about Coca Cola,Sprite or juice?

P:I don't like drinking them. What else?

Lucie:How about mineral water?

P1:Ok.

Lucie:Here you are.

P1:By the way,do you have ice cream? I want to make me cool quickly.

Lucie:Sorry,Sir. We haven't ice cream on board.

P1:Thank you all the same.

Lucie:With pleasure.

(*At the same time,a lady is waving her hand.*)

Lucie:Would you like something to drink,Madam?

P2:Yes,what have you got?

Lucie:We have hot water,tea,coffee,yogurt,and various aperitifs. Which one would you like?

P2:A cup of tea,please.

Lucie:Green tea or black tea?

P2:I prefer Pu'er tea.

Lucie:I'm awfully sorry because we don't have that on board. Is there anything else you'd like?

P2:Do you have jasmine tea?

Lucie:Yes,we have.

P2:Please give me a cup of hot jasmine tea with a little sugar.

Lucie:Ok, wait a moment. A cup of hot jasmine tea with a little sugar, here you are. Please enjoy it.

P2:Thank you very much.

Lucie:It's nothing!

(*Lucie moves on...*)

P3:Excuse me,Miss. What aperitifs have you got?

Lucie:We have Whiskey,cocktail,Johnnie Walker,wine,and Bourbon.

P3:Do you have Johnnie Walker Red Label?

Lucie:Yes. How would you like your Johnnie Walker Red Label,Sir?

P3:I'll have it with ice.

Lucie:Ok,Sir. Would you like a chaser?

P3:Just give me some water,please.

Lucie:Certainly.

P3:Do I need to pay extra fee for it?

Lucie: No. It's free of charge, Sir.

P3: Many thanks.

Lucie: I enjoyed helping you. Please wait a moment. I will get it for you as soon as possible.

Dialogue two

Setting: *Flight attendant Andrea pushes a cart up the aisle of the aircraft. She begins to serve the passengers who had ordered the special diets.*

Andrea: Excuse me, Madam. Are you Jenny?

P1: Yes, what's the matter?

Andrea: You ordered vegetarian lunch, didn't you?

P1: Yes, Miss.

Andrea: What would you like, Madam?

P1: I want to have pasta with spicy tomato sauce. What else can I have?

Andrea: Vegetable starter, soup, fruit, dessert and drinks.

P1: Vegetarian soup and dessert, please.

Andrea: Wait a moment, please. Here you are.

(*Just at this moment, a man is waving his hand.*)

P2: Excuse me, Miss. Do you have Muslim meal?

Andrea: Have you ordered in advance?

P2: No.

Andrea: Oh, Please wait a moment. I'll check in the galley. ⋯I'm very sorry, there are no more Muslim meal left for you. Perhaps a vegetarian meal is the best alternative. Would you care for it?

P2: Ok, thank you.

Andrea: I suggest you should order a special meal (kosher meal, low salt meal or diabetic meal (DBML)) when you book your ticket. For these must be pre-arranged and featured on passenger manifest. That will ensure you have correct diet.

P2: I will. Thank you for your assist.

Andrea: That's all right.

Dialogue three

Setting: *It's 8:10 a. m. (Being Standard Time). Flight C919 has entered the cruising altitude. It is time for flight attendants to serve lunch to the passengers. Flight attendant Betty pushes a cart up the aisle of the aircraft.*

Betty: Excuse me, Sir. Please put down your tray table. Lunch is coming.

P: Ah! I'm really starving now.

Betty: What would you like?

P：I have no idea. Could you recommend some to me?

Betty：Do you want to eat Chinese food or western food?

P：Western breakfast, please.

Betty：Would you like to have some hors d'oeuvres?

P：Ok. What kind of hors d'oeuvres do you have?

Betty：We have shrimp, caviar and so on.

P：I'd like to eat some Chinese delicacies.

Betty：Ok, and what would you like to follow? How about the main course?

P：What have you got?

Betty：We have fish, chicken, roast beef and pork. Which would you prefer?

P：Do you have steak?

Betty：I'm sorry, Sir. We are out of steak. Would you like to try the roast beef? It's very tender and delicious.

P：All right.

Betty：How would you like your roast beef cooked, Sir.

P：Medium well, please.

Betty：Would you like some drinks to go with your breakfast?

P：A cup of coffee, please.

Betty：How would you like your coffee, with cream, milk or sugar?

P：No, thanks. I'd like to have a cup of black coffee. Please make it very strong.

Betty：Ok, wait a moment. Here you are. By the way, what would you like for dessert? We can serve you fresh fruit salad with cream or some cakes.

P：A piece of cake, please.

Betty：Ok, please enjoy it.

P：Thank you for your kindness.

Betty：It's my pleasure.

Words and Expressions

alcoholic /ˌælkəˈhɔlik/	a.	酒精的
captain /ˈkæptin/	n.	机长
thirsty /ˈθəːsti/	a.	口渴的
cart /kɑːt/	n.	手推车
Sprite /sprait/	n.	雪碧
juice /dʒuːs/	n.	果汁
mineral water /ˈminərəl/		矿泉水
trolley /ˈtrɔli/	n.	手推车
yogurt /ˈjəʊgət/	n.	酸奶

aperitif /ə'peritiːf/	n.	开胃酒
awfully /'ɔːfli/	ad.	很，非常
jasmine /'dʒæzmin/	n.	茉莉花
whisky /'wiski/	n.	威士忌酒
Johnnie Walker Red Label		尊尼获加（威士忌）红牌
chaser /'tʃeisə/	n.	饮烈酒后喝的饮料(如姜汁酒、啤酒或凉开水等)
extra /'ekstrə/	a.	额外的
charge /tʃɑːdʒ/	n.	费用
vegetarian /ˌvedʒɪ'teəriən/	n.	素食者
pasta /'pɑːstə/	n.	意大利面食
spicy /'spaisi/	a.	辛辣的
sauce /sɔːs/	n.	调味汁
starter /starter/	n.	（主菜之前的）开胃品
dessert /di'zəːt/	n.	甜食
Muslim /'muslim/	a.	穆斯林的
galley /'gæliː/	n.	（航空器上的）厨房
alternative /ɔːl'təːnətiv/	n.	可供选择的事物
kosher /'kəuʃə/	a.	犹太教食品
diabetic /ˌdaiə'betik/	a.	糖尿病的
DBML（diabetic meal）		糖尿病人餐品
manifest /'mænifest/	n.	旅客名单
recommend /ˌrekə'mend/	v.	推荐，介绍
continental breakfast		欧式早餐
hors d'oeuvres /ˌɔː'dəːvz/	n.	开胃小吃
shrimp /ʃrimp/	n.	小虾
caviar /'kævɪɑː/	n.	鱼子酱
main course		主菜
roast beef		烤牛肉
steak /steik/	n.	牛排
tender /'tendə/	a.	嫩的
delicious / di'liʃəs/	a.	美味的
medium well /'miːdiəm/		（牛排等的熟度）七分熟的

Exercises

1. Questions for discussion.

1) How do the flight attendants tell the passengers what drinks are available?

2) How does a flight attendant do if a passenger is sleeping while serving meal?

3) How should you say to a passenger if the passenger wants a cup of coffee, but there isn't boiled water on board now?

4) If a passenger wants to have Muslim meal, yet he doesn't book in advance. What should you say to the passengers?

5) A passenger wants a tin of beer that has been out of stock on board. How will you say to the passenger?

2. Oral Practice.

Work with a partner to make up dialogues. Situational settings are as follows:

1) A passenger complains why you don't offer any drinks for a long time.

2) A passenger wants to drink hot beverages, but you can not serve hot drinks on the flight because the water system is out of order. Please explain to the passenger.

Section B   Announcements

Drink service（I）

Ladies and Gentlemen,

May we have your attention, please? Our plane has entered the cruising altitude. The illuminated seat belts have been switched off, so you may move around the cabin if needed. However, we suggest you keep your seat belt fastened when you're seated. You may turn on your electronic devices such as laptop and iPad, yet your mobile phones must be switched off during the whole flight.

We will be offering you all kinds of drinks shortly. Please put down your tray table in front of you. We offer alcoholic and non-alcoholic drinks on the flight. All non-alcoholic drinks such as coffee, tea, juice, Coca cola, Seven-up, Pepsi, yogurt and so on are free for every passenger, but some alcoholic drinks such as Dynasty, Chivas Regal and Whisky are needed to pay extra fare. If you have special diet requirement, please don't hesitate to contact us. We'll try to provide you with the best quality service.

Thank you!

Meal service（II）

Ladies and Gentlemen,

We are pleased to begin our meal service. Flight attendants will be moving through the cabin serving meals (snacks) and beverages soon. Please put down the tray table in front of you. For the convenience of the passenger sitting behind you, please adjust your seat back to its upright position during the meal service. If you need any assistance, please contact any flight attendant. Our crew members will make every effort to provide you with the best service. Enjoy the flight.

Thank you!

Meal service（III）

Good Morning Ladies and Gentlemen，

We will be offering you meal with hot or cold drinks. For today's lunch，we have prepared for Chinese food and western food for all passengers. We can also provide special meals such as vegetarian，vegan，and kosher. But these have been pre-arranged when booking the flight ticket and the passenger's names have been listed so that our flight attendants can identify and serve the special meals during the flight. Thus you can't get the specific diets on board if you haven't booked in advance. Thank you for your understanding.

Words and Expressions

switch off		关闭，切断
tray /trei/	n.	托盘
Seven-up	n.	七喜
Pepsi /ˈpepsi/	n.	百事可乐
Dynasty /ˈdainəsti/	n.	皇朝酒
Chivas Regal	n.	芝华士酒
fare /fɛə/	n.	费用
diet /ˈdaiət/	n.	饮食
snack /snæk/	n.	小吃，点心
convenience /kənˈviːniəns/	n.	方便
effort /ˈefət/	n.	努力
vegan /ˈvedʒən/	n.	纯素主义者(既不吃也不用任何动物产品,如蛋、丝绸、皮革)
identify /aiˈdentifai/	v.	鉴定；识别
specific /spəˈsɪfɪk/	a.	特定类别的,具体的

Exercises

1. Match the English phrases in column A with the Chinese translations in column B.

A	B
（　）a. Hainan Airlines（H4）	1）新加坡航空公司
（　）b. Japan Airlines（JL）	2）大韩航空公司
（　）c. Singapore Airlines（SQ）	3）海南航空公司
（　）d. Thai Airways International（TG）	4）日本航空公司
（　）e. Korean Airlines（KE）	5）泰国国际航空公司
（　）f. Alitalia Airlines（AZ）	6）新西兰航空公司
（　）g. Canadian International Airlines（AC）	7）马来西亚航空公司
（　）h. Malaysian Airlines	8）加拿大国际航空公司

(　　) i. New Zealand Airways(NZ) 9）深圳航空公司

(　　) j. Shenzhen Airlines(4G) 10）意大利航空公司

2. Translate the following sentences into English.

1）女士，您好！请问您想喝点什么？咖啡、果汁还是热茶？

2）本次航班我们为您提供以下冷饮：矿泉水、果汁、雪碧、可乐，热饮包括咖啡、红茶和热水，都有供应。

3）先生，您好！您还需要再来点饮料吗？

4）我们不接受小费的，为乘客服务是我们的义务。谢谢您了。

5）非常抱歉。我们飞机上没有咖啡了。您来点绿茶怎么样？

6）您想要几分熟的牛排？嫩点的、适中的还是老点的？

7）这是今天的菜单，您想吃点什么？

8）午餐想吃鸡肉、牛肉还是鱼肉？

9）请把您的小桌板打开，午餐来了。

10）请问您用完餐了吗？可以清理您的托盘吗？

3. Translate the following sentences into Chinese.

1）Excuse me, Miss. When will you serve the drinks? I'm a little bit thirsty.

2）What kind of drinks do you have?

3）Would you tell me when you are going to serve lunch?

4）I've asked for a cup of coffee three times. How long will I have to wait?

5）We are sorry to inform you that we can't serve you hot drinks now.

6）Excuse me, Miss. When will we have dinner? I've already felt hungry.

7）I want beef rice, but not chicken noodles.

8）Delicious food and excellent service have left a deep impression on me during the whole flight.

9）I enjoy the dinner very much. The beef is very fresh and tender.

10）Excuse me, Sir. Because I can't eat pork, I had ordered Muslim meal. When will my lunch be served?

4. Suppose you are a flight attendant. Now you are serving drinks on board. Please fill in the blanks of the following dialogue.

FA：Excuse me, Sir. What would you like to drink?

P：What have you got?

FC：(1)_____.

P：A cup of coffee, please.

FA：How do you like your coffee, with milk or sugar?

P：(2)_____.

FA: Well, wait a moment, please. Here you are.

P: (3) _____ .

FA: Not at all. Anything more?

P: Er... I'm a little hungry. When will you serve dinner?

FA: (4) _____ .

P: May I have another cup of orange juice?

FA: (5) _____ .

5. Fill in the blanks in the following sentences with the words given below. Change the form where necessary.

diet remind available fare entire
provide prohibit awfully prefer switch

1) The government _____ emergency accommodation for the homeless.

2) You will be informed when the book is _____ .

3) Don't forget to _____ off the gas when you leave home.

4) You look _____ pale. Are you ill now?

5) She _____ walking to cycling.

6) The law _____ tobacconists from selling cigarettes to children.

7) She always _____ myself that time and tide wait for no man.

8) Air traveler is complained about rising _____ .

9) We must _____ and take more exercise.

10) Although they are twins, they look _____ different.

6. Complete the paragraph with the correct word in the box.

choice effort attention press put
return cabin trip diet convenience

Ladies and Gentlemen:

May we have your 1) _____ , please? After a while, our flight attendants will be walking around the 2) _____ to serve you meal with hot water, coffee, juice, tea and other soft drinks. Welcome to make your 3) _____ . Please 4) _____ down the tray table in front of you. For the 5) _____ of the passenger behind you, please 6) _____ your seat back to the upright position during the meal service. If you have special 7) _____ requirements, please 8) _____ your call button to identify yourself. Our crew members will make every 9) _____ to provide you with the best service. Hope to have a good 10) _____ !

Thank you!

Section C   Supplementary Reading

A Guide to Airline Meals and Snacks

Even if you fly regularly, it can be difficult to keep track of what food might be available in the air these days. The days of complimentary airline meals on U. S. domestic flights are long gone, but a couple of carriers have recently begun to offer free snacks, and many others offer a variety of goodies for purchase. If you'd like to be prepared for what food will be available to you on your next flight, see meal and snack options on some of the most popular U. S. carriers.

If you're flying in business or first class (except on very short flights), or on an overseas international flight, you can usually assume there will be a variety of dining choices. However, it's always worth checking ahead.

Alaska Airlines

Alaska Airlines sells hot meals on flights over 2. 5 hours; a fruit and cheese platter is available for purchase on most flights over two hours. Prices range from $7 to $8. Snacks known as"picnic packs"cost $6. There's a special selection of for-purchase meals on flights to and from Hawaii, including red miso ginger chicken ($7).

Non-alcoholic beverages are complimentary, while beer, wine and liquors cost $6 to $7 in economy class (they're free in first).

American Airlines

American Airlines recently began offering free snacks in economy class on all domestic flights (cookies or pretzels), as well as free meals on flights between Dallas/Fort Worth and Hawaii. Complimentary meals are also offered aboard flights between the U. S. and Europe, Asia and some destinations in Latin America.

On other international flights as well as all domestic flights, economy-class fliers can purchase items such as snack packs, sandwiches and other light fare ($4 ~ $9.99). Passengers in first or business class get free snacks,"Lite Bites"or full meals, depending on the length and time of the flight.

Non-alcoholic beverages are free on all flights, while economy-class passengers will pay $7 to $9 for alcoholic options. (These are free in business and first class.)

Delta

Delta offers one complimentary snack (pretzels, peanuts or cookies) on most economy-class flights, as well as a menu of for-purchase items such as Pringles chips, sandwiches, wraps and fruit/cheese plates ($3.49~$9.99) on U.S. Caribbean and Latin America flights of at least 900 miles. Complimentary meals are available on longer international flights.

First-class and business-class passengers get complimentary snacks or meals, depending on the length of the flight.

Complimentary non-alcoholic drinks are offered on all flights. First and business-class passengers get free alcoholic drinks, while economy-class passengers pay $6 to $10.

United

United offers complimentary meals in coach on most international flights. In coach class on North American flights over two hours (including flights to the continental U.S., Alaska, Hawaii, Canada, Central America, the Caribbean and Mexico), snacks are available for purchase for $3.99 to $8.99. On Northern American flights over 3.5 hours, fliers can purchase more substantive options such as sandwiches and salads ($5.99~$9.99).

In first or business class, meals and snacks are complimentary and vary based on the length of your flight and the time of day.

On all flights, soft drinks are complimentary; economy-class passengers pay $6.99 to $9.99 for alcoholic beverages, while passengers in the premium cabin enjoy these for free.

Virgin America

Virgin America charges $3 to $5 for all snacks in economy class, and $4 to $9 for meals such as sandwiches or salads. Most of these items are complimentary in first class or Main Cabin Select (premium economy). Meals are available on all flights over two hours.

Some non-alcoholic beverages are free (such as Coke, Sprite, orange juice and coffee), while "premium" non-alcoholic drinks (including some teas) are $2 to $3 in coach. Alcoholic drinks range from $6 to $8 for economy-class fliers. Fliers in premium cabins enjoy most drinks for free.

Questions for discussion.

1. What airline sells hot meals on flights? And how much does the price range?
2. What service does American Airlines offer in the economy class on all domestic flights?
3. Are non-alcoholic drinks available to all the passengers aboard in Delta?
4. Which one doesn't serve meals but snacks among all the airlines mentioned in the passage?
5. How much are the "premium" non-alcoholic drinks in Virgin America?

Section D　Interview English

Daily hot topic：

Reasons for applying

The typical questions on daily hot topic have been usually asked when you attend an interview. There are several examples. The answers are given for your reference.

1. Why do you choose our airline?

A：I know something about your airline. Your airline enjoys good reputation. Furthermore, I like your work environment which is very friendly and harmonious.

2. Why are you interested in working as a flight attendant?

A：My major is cabin service, so working as a flight attendant could give me the best chance to use what I have learnt at school. What's more, I think the most important thing is my interest in the job.

3. Do you think you are able to qualify with this job?

A：Sure. I have full confidence and competence to qualify with this job, so I have the interview now. I hope you would give a chance to let me prove my ability.

4. Why should I choose you over all the others?

A：As I have said, my character is suitable to work as a flight attendant. I also like teamwork and enjoy working with all kinds of people. You can trust me 100% to do well on all the tasks you assign me.

5. What made you decide to work as a flight attendant?

A：When I was a child, I imagined flying into the blue sky some day. Therefore, now I think the day has come. My dream will come true. I like this job which is full of challenges. Because I will communicate with different people everyday, the job isn't dull. All in all I like this job.

Role-play practice：

You want to be a flight attendant and have an interview. The interviewer asks you whether you have considered the difficulties that this job will cause you. Please make an interview role-play with your partner.

Unit 6

Special Passengers Service

Lead-in questions

1. What should (not) a flight attendant do during the process of first aid?

2. How will you do to help a passenger whose life is in danger?

3. What will you do if you see a physically disabled passenger boarding?

Section A Dialogues

Dialogue one

Setting: A young girl presses the call button. A flight attendant named Lily goes there to see what the matter is.

(P: passenger)

Lily: Excuse me, Miss. Did you press the call button? What's the matter with you?

P: I'm feeling uncomfortable and dizzy. Would you like to help me?

Lily: Don't worry. From my experience you are probably airsick. Have you ever suffered from airsickness before?

P:Oh,it's my first time to take an aircraft. I have no idea. What should I do with it?

Lily:I will bring some airsick tablets and a glass of hot water to you. You'd better take the medicine and have a rest.

P:Thank you. By the way,where can I vomit? I feel a little nauseous now.

Lily:You may use the airsickness bag in the seat pocket in front of you.

Lily:Your hot water and tablets,please. If you still feel bad,please don't hesitate to call us.

(*After a while,the young girl presses the call button again,Lily comes to her.*)

Lily:Do you feel better now?

P:It's too terrible. I began to vomit after taking the medicine.

Lily:I'm very sorry to hear that. I suggest you'd better take a tablet once again since you have thrown it up.

P:But I think it's useless taking that medicine.

Lily:The medicine doesn't work so quickly. It usually takes effect in one hour.

P:I see,so I have to take the medicine for airsickness once more.

Lily:Yes. Here you are. You will feel better soon. We have some empty seats in the front of the cabin. If you'd like to take a nap,I can lift up the armrests and let you lie down.

P:How considerate of you! I'm pleased to hear that. By the way, why do I feel earache? Is it the symptom of airsickness?

Lily:No,this symptom is common during the flight. You can just relieve the earache by chewing gums or eating something else. If it's no use,I can tell you another way. You firstly draw a deep breath, and stop your nose with the fingers and try to blow your nose. Please follow me to do it. You may have a try.

P:Ok,I really can't thank you enough for everything you've done for me.

Lily:It's my pleasure to serve you well.

Dialogue two

Setting:A cabin attendant called Monica stands at the cabin to welcome passengers. At this time,she finds that a blind man is entering the cabin along with a guide dog.

Monica:Excuse me, Sir. Would you like to show me your boarding pass? I'd like to take you to your seat.

P1:Sure,here you are. Thank you.

Monica:It's 16C,please give me your hand,I'll lead you to your seat.

P1:Many thanks.

Monica:You are welcome.

P1:Then how about my guide dog? Can it stay with me here?

Monica: Yes, it can. The dog can sit at your feet as long as you have enough legroom.

P1: Do I need pay extra fee for it?

Monica: Of course not.

P1: Ok, thank you.

Monica: Not at all. May I help you put your handbag in the overhead compartment?

P1: Yeah.

Monica: Do you need pillow and blanket? I can bring them for you.

P1: Ok, I just want to take a nap after a while. By the way, may I get something to drink? I'm too thirsty.

Monica: Of course, what would you want to drink?

P1: A cup of coffee without sugar. And make it very strong, please.

Monica: I see. Wait a moment, please. No sugar, straight coffee and very black. Here you are. Please enjoy it.

P1: Thanks.

Monica: If you need my help, please don't hesitate to call me.

(*Monica says to the passenger next to the blind man.*)

Monica: Excuse me, Sir. Would you like to help him press the call button if he needs my help?

P2: No problem. But where is the call button?

Monica: It's on the side of your armrest. It's here.

P2: I know.

Monica: Thank you for your kindness.

P2: Don't mention it.

Exercises

1. Questions for discussion.

1) What will you do if there is a heart attack passenger on board?

2) How do you give a special service for a blind passenger with a guide dog?

3) How will you help a passenger if he feels uncomfortable in his ears?

4) How do you provide a special service for an unaccompanied child?

5) There is no doctor or nurse on board. What can you do to assist an airsick passenger?

2. Oral Practice.

Work with a partner to make up dialogues. Situational settings are as follows:

1) A passenger presses the call button. She wants to get some medicine for his cold. You ask her to describe her symptom. From your experience, she is airsick instead of getting a cold.

2) A passenger suffers from a heart attack. After taking some medicine, it's even

worse. There are no medical professionals on board, while the passenger's life is in danger. So at this time, the captain decides to make an emergency landing. You tell the sick passenger you have contacted the ground crew and everything is ready.

Words and Expressions

first aid		急救
physically disabled		残疾人
airsick /eəˈsik/	*a.*	晕机的
vomit /ˈvɔmit/	*v.*	呕吐
nauseous /ˈnɔːziːəs/	*a.*	恶心的，令人作呕的
throw up		呕吐
take a nap		小睡一下
considerate /kənˈsidərit/	*a.*	体贴的
symptom /ˈsimptəm/	*n.*	症状
chew /tʃu/	*v.*	咀嚼
gum /gʌm/	*n.*	口香糖
guide dog		导盲犬
legroom /ˈledruːm/	*n.*	供伸腿的空间(在飞机……)
straight /streit/	*a.*	纯的；不掺其他东西的
straight coffee		纯咖啡

Section B   Announcements

Announcement（I）

Ladies and gentlemen,

Could you give me your full attention please? There is a sick passenger. If there is a doctor or a nurse on board, please contact one of the flight attendants as soon as possible.

Thank you!

Announcement（II）

May I have your attention please? There is a passenger with severe heart attack on board. The captain has decided to make an emergency landing at _____ airport in order to ensure his safety. We are expected to arrive there in twenty minutes. We apologize for any inconvenience. Your kind understanding and cooperation will be very much appreciated.

Thank you!

Words and expressions

appreciate /əˈpriːʃieit/	*v.*	感激

Exercises

1. Match the English phrases in column A with the Chinese translations in column B.

A	B
( ) a. South African Airways（SA）	1）急救
( ) b. Malaysia Airlines（MH）	2）小憩
( ) c. Take a nap	3）咽喉炎
( ) d. Transworld Airlines（TW）	4）呕吐袋
( ) e. China Eastern Airlines（MU）	5）导盲犬
( ) f. soar throat	6）环球航空公司
( ) g. airsick bag	7）马来西亚航空公司
( ) h. first aid	8）中国东方航空公司
( ) i. physically disabled	9）残疾人
( ) j. guide dog	10）南非航空公司

2. Translate the following sentences into English.

1）别担心，您试着嘴里嚼个口香糖缓解一下您的耳鸣。

2）我想吃完药过一会儿您就会好多了，请您休息一会儿吧。

3）女士您好，如果您想睡觉，为了安全您最好系好安全带。

4）各位旅客请注意。飞机上有一名突发疾病的乘客，如果机上有医生或护士，请立刻与机组人员取得联系。

5）清洁袋放在您前面的椅袋里，如果您感到恶心就用上它。

6）我帮您拿条毯子和枕头，休息一会儿，可能你会感到好些。

7）恐怕我有点晕机，你能帮我拿些晕机药吗？

8）我们已通知了地面工作人员，一到机场他们就会带您去医院。

9）真是非常感谢您为我做的一切。

10）打扰一下，女士。我仍感到恶心和不舒服，你能帮我一下吗？

3. Translate the following sentences into Chinese.

1）I have a serious stomachache. Do you have painkillers on board?

2）I seem to catch a bad cold now. My nose is stuffed up, what's more I have a headache.

3）I want to go to the lavatory. Could you supply me with a wheelchair?

4）I just feel a little dizzy and nauseous. Can you bring me a glass of hot water?

5）Don't worry, I will look for a doctor by making an announcement and arrange an ambulance upon arriving at the airport.

6）Would you like to describe your symptom? Maybe I can solve the problem on board.

7）The airsickness bag is in your seat pocket in front of you. If you feel nauseous, you may use it.

8）I feel a pain in my chest, dizzy and it's hard for me to breathe.

9) There are some vacant seats in the front cabin. I can take out the armrests and you can lie down.

10) There's a serious sick passenger on board, so the captain has decided to make an emergency landing at Hangzhou airport.

4. Suppose you are a flight attendant. Now a passenger is suffering from airsickness. He presses the call button. Please fill in the blanks of the following dialogue.

FA: Excuse me, Sir. Do you press the call button? What can I do for you?

P: I'm feeling dizzy and want to vomit. Could you help me?

FA: (1) _____.

P: (2) _____.

FA: Don't worry. Let me give you some medicine and a cup of hot water.

P: By the way, I feel painful in my ears after take-off. How do I relieve my earache?

FA: (3) _____.

P: (4) _____.

FA: Do you need any special assistance?

P: (5) _____.

5. Fill in the blanks in the following sentences with the words given below. Change the form where necessary.

symptom	appreciate	nauseous	contact	considerate
terrible	emergency	disabled	ensure	swallow

1) You can only use this door in an _____ .

2) The _____ thunderstorm destroyed many houses in the town.

3) Young eagles soon learn to kill and _____ even large snakes.

4) A group of young pioneers always accompany the _____ boy to the school.

5) This demonstration was a _____ of discontent among the workers.

6) This medicine will _____ you a good night's sleep.

7) You can't _____ English poetry unless you understand its rhythm.

8) I'll get in _____ with a rental car company.

9) Have you been _____ or vomiting recently?

10) It was very _____ of you to send me a postcard.

6. Complete the paragraph with the correct word in the box.

cross	route	carry	beverages	button
located	prohibited	remind	provinces	rear

Ladies and Gentlemen:

Our plane was from Guangzhou to Beijing. On this air 1) _____ we will be passing over the 2) _____ of Guangdong, Hunan, Hubei, Henan, and Hebei. And we'll 3) _____ the Yellow River and Yangtse River. This plane is a Boeing 737-

800. It can 4) _____ 260 passengers. The reading light and call 5) _____ are above your head. Toilets are 6) _____ in the front and the 7) _____ part of the cabin. We 8) _____ you that this is a non-smoking flight. Smoking is 9) _____ on the entire aircraft, including the toilets. We'll be serving refreshments and 10) _____ soon.

Wish you a good trip! Thank you.

Section C Supplementary Reading

Vulnerable Passengers

The airline may be able to let you board first or last depending on what would be most beneficial and possibly seat you either in the front or back row of the plane where there is often more room. This would enable you to disembark the aircraft as quickly as possible upon landing. Please speak with a member of staff at the gate and explain that you or the person you are travelling with experiences issues with crowds due to their particular condition, staff will always try to help when they can.

Remember to give the airline advance notice if there are any special dietary requirements, particularly if someone is following the gluten or casein-free diet as this may take longer to organize.

Sometimes coming to visit the airport to have a look around before the day you travel can help, especially with young children. You will be able to see the check in desks and also view the security area.

Ensure children or vulnerable adults have identification cards. This can be discreetly pinned onto their clothing if needed. Please include a mobile contact number for yourself.

At security we've created special assistance lanes for both departing and arriving families. Our separate security lane gives families travelling with young children and vulnerable passengers more time when passing through the security checks. Simply follow the signs for assistance lanes or ask a member of staff who will be able to direct you towards the correct area. Please advise staff of any relevant condition when arriving in the assistance lane so we can do our best to help you.

Following on from the success of our security assistance lanes, we've also introduced assistance lanes through border control to help families arriving back at Gatwick. Our staff will be on hand during busy times to give some extra help.

If you would like to wait in the quietest surroundings possible we have lounges that can be booked in advance. There is a charge to use the lounges as they also include complimentary food and drink. Please see the lounges section of our website for more information on these facilities.

If you have a hearing or sight impairment, please explain this to the cabin crew on the plane so that they can keep you informed of any important announcements such as delays or emergency landings.

Travelling with Children

You can take an additional item of hand baggage even when travelling with a child who has no seat assigned to them, but please do always check baggage restrictions with your airline.

Baby milks in containers over 100ml can pass though security when travelling with a baby but half of the containers will need to be opened and tested, so please keep this in mind if travelling with cartons. The milk doesn't need to go inside the clear plastic bag provided at security, however all other liquids, gels and pastes need to be placed in the bag. The plastic bag must be sealed and you can take one bag per passenger. Please place the bag into the tray with your other items.

You may carry milk powder and there are no limits for how much of this you can take.

Wet wipes are fine but all baby creams and lotions are included in the 100ml regulation.

You can buy ready-to-drink infant formula after security from Boots and this can be ordered in advance by calling: 01293 569606 (North Terminal) and 01293 569353 (South Terminal). Pack extra snacks, drinks, coloring books, crayons and their favorite cuddly toy.

At security if travelling with two adults, one adult can walk through the archway metal detector first so the child can see what to do. The child can then meet their parent on the other side once they have walked through the archway metal detector.

To help your child cope with the aircraft noise during take-off and landing you may consider using some headphones. There are also headphones which have been designed to shut out all surrounding noise including the sounds of aircraft engines.

It's likely that your baby will need a passport and a ticket if you are travelling internationally, please double check to ensure that your baby is covered by your travel insurance.

Most airlines do have sky cots on the aircraft however they are not always available and are only available in a few sections of the aircraft. Please speak with your airline before you travel if you are concerned.

Please ask a flight attendant about heating up bottles or providing hot water, or if you don't have a cooler bag and need something chilled please ask for ice. We can't guarantee your airline will be able to provide these services, so please check in advance.

Questions for discussion.

1. What should you do if you have special dietary requirements?

2. What are special security assistance lanes used for?

3. Who should you turn to help if you have a hearing or sight impairment?

4. Who is advised to walk through the archway metal detector first, at security if children are travelling with two adults?

5. How do you help your child cope with the aircraft noise during take-off and landing?

Section D   Interview English

Daily hot topic:

College life

The typical questions on daily hot topic have been usually asked when you attend an interview. There are several examples. The answers are given for your reference.

1. How do you like your college?

A: It's a good comprehensive university. Teachers are all knowledgeable and responsible for all students. New flight simulator and multi-media classrooms are all introduced into the college and the campus environment is very beautiful.

2. Would you describe your college life?

A: My college life is rich and colorful. Besides the stressful curriculum, I made many friends by taking part in extracurricular activities, which made me get social experience. I think my college life is my best memory.

3. How are your grades in college?

A: I was doing very well in college. I was one of the top students in the class. I could make good use of the study time. / My school record is average in my class, yet I think I have strong leadership and organization skill. A student who can achieve high scores isn't sure to have high capabilities. I think my comprehensive ability is strong.

4. What was your favorite subject in college? Why?

A: My favorite subject is English for airline flight attendant. After learning it, I know how to communicate with the foreigners and how to serve them well. I learned a lot from the course.

5. What do you think of the college education in your life?

A: I think my college was worth it, I learned a lot during the college. I have not only learned some knowledge but also improved my communication ability. College education was a good opportunity for me to broaden our horizon. Therefore, it was the most wonderful experience in my life.

Role-play practice:

You want to be a flight attendant and have an interview. The interviewer asks you which band you have passed in College English Test and how your scores are at college. Please make an interview role-play with your partner.

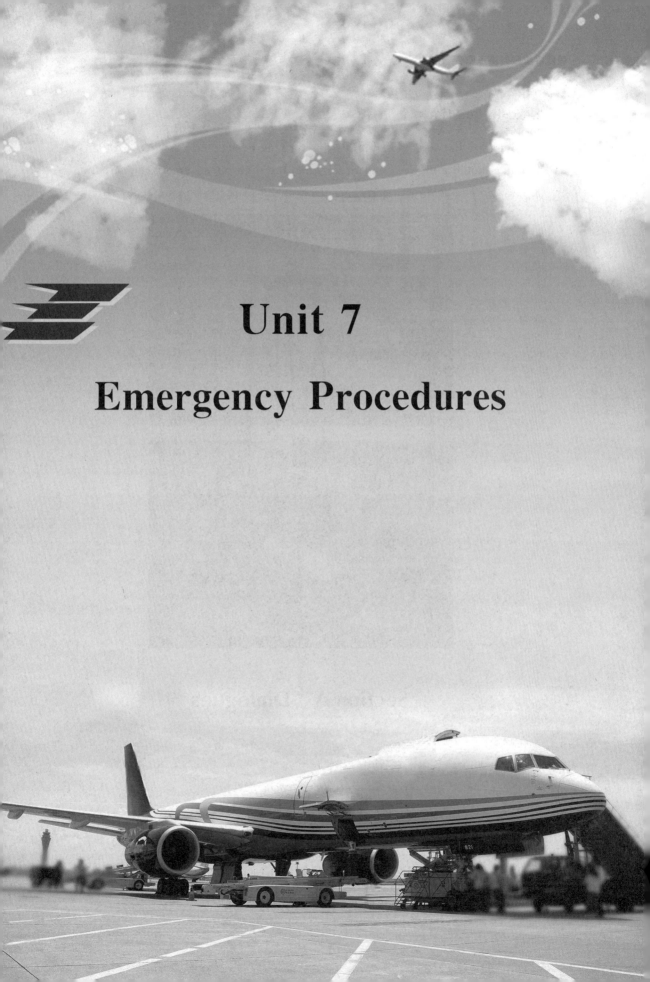

Unit 7

Emergency Procedures

Lead-in questions

1. Could you list some possible reasons for emergency landings?

2. What should a flight attendant do when the flight meets emergency situation?

3. How do you comfort a passenger if he/she is scared in an emergency situation?

Section A   Dialogues

Dialogue one

Setting：The flight meets a severe turbulence. The plane is shaking terribly. Flight attendant Laura tries to comfort the passengers.

(P：*passenger*)

P：Excuse me，Miss. Why is the plane shaking terribly? It makes me very uncomfortable.

Laura：I'm sorry to say that we hit some unexpected turbulence. Please remain your seatbelts fastened and don't move along the aisle.

P:I wonder whether the turbulence is severe. What should we do now? I'm a little scared.

Laura:Don't panic! Our captain has full competence to deal with it. All the crew members of this flight are well trained for this kind of situation. So please follow our instructions.

P:Ok.

(*Ten minutes later, the plane flies normally. Then there comes a cabin announcement.*)

Laura:Ladies and Gentlemen, although we met a severe turbulence just now, our experienced captain has dealt with the difficulties successfully. So you needn't worry about if now. Yet I am sorry to inform you that the flight will land at an alternate airport due to the unfavorable weather conditions over Shanghai Pudong International Airport. We do apologize for any inconvenience and appreciate your understanding.

P:Excuse me, Miss. Where will we land?

Laura:We will land at Hangzhou Xiaoshan International Airport ten minutes later. We will stay there until the weather conditions improve. Further information will be given soon.

P:What are the unfavorable weather conditions?

Laura:The visibility in Shanghai Pudong International Airport is lower than the standard required by CAAC, so our flight is not allowed to land.

P:Oh, I see. But I will attend a conference in Shanghai tomorrow. How can I go there?

Laura:If only we receive the instructions permitted to fly over Shanghai Pudong International Airport, we will take off as soon as possible. I believe it won't affect your conference.

P:That's ok.

Laura:I'm very sorry for that. I sincerely hope you can understand me.

P:Well, I see. Thank you.

Dialogue two

Setting:The Plane will make an emergency ditching because of oil leakage from the aircraft. All the crew members of this flight are arranging the passengers to evacuate. A passenger with a child pushes the call button.

FA:Excuse me, Madam. Is there anything I can do for you?

P:Sir, I'm too nervous and scared. I can't find life vests for my son. Would you like to help me?

FA:Don't be nervous. First you should be seated and remain your seatbelt fastened. I'll take the life vest from the overhead compartment for you. Here you are.

P:Thanks a lot.

FA:You put on your life vest quickly. It's under your seat. I'll help your son to put it on.

P：Ok. May I inflate the life vest now?

FA：No，Madam.

P：Why not? It may be too late to inflate it outside the cabin.

FA：There will be no room inside the cabin if all passengers inflate their life vests. What's more，some sharp objects may damage the life vest on the way out.

P：I see.

FA：When you hear the brace command，please bend over more，place your head between your knees and hold your ankles. Meanwhile，you should help your son to finish the action.

P：Ok. Sorry，Sir. Just now I was so nervous that I didn't see the use of oxygen mask clearly. Could you show me how to use it again?

FA：Sure，look，please pull the oxygen mask over your nose and mouth and breathe normally. Are you clear?

P：Well.

（The plane has landed safely. All passengers are evacuating. A passenger is crying "help".）

P：Help… help me.

FA：What's up?

P：I can't release my seatbelt! Save me quickly.

FA：Ok，let me help you. Please leave the cabin quickly.

P：Can you get my handbag from the overhead bin?

FA：Leave your bags behind…go…go…quickly.

P：Where is the exit? I can't see anything.

FA：In the front. Hold onto the person in front of you，and follow him to the exit. Please remove your high-heel shoes and glasses.

P：My glasses! I need glasses.

FA：Remove your glasses. It's dangerous when using the emergency escape chute.

P：Ok. Too horrible!

Words and Expressions

comfort /ˈkʌmfət/	v.	安慰，抚慰
scared /skeəd/	a.	惊慌的
panic /ˈpænik/	v.	恐慌
competence /ˈkɔmpitəns/	n.	能力，技能
instruction /inˈstrʌkʃən/	n.	命令，指示
alternate /ɔːlˈtəːnət/	a.	代替的
alternate airport		备用航空站

visibility /ˌvizəˈbilitiː/	n.	能见度
conference /ˈkɔnfərəns/	n.	会议,研讨会
influence /ˈinfluəns/	v.	影响
ditching /ˈditʃiŋ/	n.	水上迫降
leakage /ˈliːkidʒ/	n.	漏,漏出
evacuate /iˈvækjueit/	v.	撤离,疏散
damage /ˈdæmidʒ/	v.	损害,毁坏
brace /breis/	v.	支住,撑牢
command /kəˈmɑːnd/	v.	命令,指挥
ankle /ˈæŋkl/	n.	脚踝
release /riˈliːs/	v.	释放;松开
remove /riˈmuːv/	v.	脱去(衣服等),摘下
escape /isˈkeip/	n.	逃脱,逃跑
chute /ʃuːt/	n.	斜槽,滑道

Exercises

1. Questions for discussion.

1) How do you teach passengers to inflate their life vest?

2) How do you teach passengers to use their oxygen mask?

3) What should you do if the plane makes an emergency ditching at once?

4) How should a passenger deal with his carry-on baggage in the event of an emergency?

5) What do you ask the passengers to do in preparation for landing at an alternate airport?

2. Oral Practice.

Work with a partner to make up dialogues. Situational settings are as follows:

1) The plane will make an emergency ditching because of the sudden breakdown of an engine. You arrange all the passengers to evacuate.

2) The plane will make an emergency landing because of a sick passenger whose life is in danger. You try to explain to the other passengers. Maybe they will stay there overnight.

Section B   Announcements

Emergency landing/ditching

Ladies and Gentlemen,

Attention please! It is necessary to make an emergency landing. The crew have been well trained to handle this situation. We will make every effort to ensure your safety and keep calm, pay close attention to the flight attendants and follow their instructions.

Please pass your food tray and all other service items for pick up.

Please put the high-heeled shoes, dentures, necklaces, ties, pens, earrings, watches and jewelry in the overhead bin or hand them to the flight attendants.

Fasten your seat belt, bring your seat backs to the upright position and stow all tray tables. Stow footrests and in-seat video units. Please put all of your baggage under the seat in front of you or in the overhead compartment.

(Now the flight attendants will explain the use of life vest. Please put your life vest on and follow the instructions of your flight attendants.)

Now the flight attendants are pointing to the exits nearest to you. Please identify them and be aware your closest exit may be behind you. When evacuating, leave everything on board!

Now we will explain you brace position against impact. When instructed to brace against impact, put your legs apart, place your feet flat on the floor. Cross your arms like this, lean forward as far as possible, hold the seat back in front of you and rest your face on your arms.

(When instructed to brace against impact, cross your arms above your head, then bend over, keep your head down, stay down.)

Thank you for your cooperation.

Cautions

Ladies and Gentlemen,

Attention please! This is your chief purser speaking. We will be landing in 5 minutes. As there may be two or more impacts on touchdown, you should brace against impact when the captain orders. Please keep your brace position until the plane comes to a complete stop and then follow the instructions of the flight attendants to proceed to emergency evacuation. Don't carry any baggage during emergency evacuation. Please help the flight attendants to make preparation.

Thank you very much.

Words and Expressions

high-heeled /ˈhaiˈhiːld/	a.	高跟的
denture /ˈdentʃə/	n.	假牙
necklace /ˈneklis/	n.	项链
tie /tai/	n.	领带
earring /ˌiəˈriŋ/	n.	耳环
jewelry /ˈdʒuːəlri/	n.	珠宝

aware /əˈweə/　　　　　　　　　　　　　*a.*　意识到的，知晓的

impact /ˈimpækt/　　　　　　　　　　　*n.*　碰撞；冲击；撞击

apart /əˈpɑːt/　　　　　　　　　　　　*ad.*　分离着

flat /flæt/　　　　　　　　　　　　　　*ad.*　水平地；直接地，完全地

touchdown /ˈtʌtʃˌdaun/　　　　　　　　*n.*　着陆；降落

proceed /prəˈsiːd/　　　　　　　　　　*v.*　进行；继续下去

Exercises

1. Match the English phrases in column A with the Chinese translations in column B.

<table>
<tr><td align="center">A</td><td align="center">B</td></tr>
<tr><td>(　　) a. Okay Airways(BK)</td><td>1) 紧急撤离</td></tr>
<tr><td>(　　) b. Air Belgium(AJ)</td><td>2) 华夏航空公司(中国)</td></tr>
<tr><td>(　　) c. China Express Air(G5)</td><td>3) 救生衣</td></tr>
<tr><td>(　　) d. Hong Kong Dragon Air(KA)</td><td>4) 紧急迫降</td></tr>
<tr><td>(　　) e. Swiss Air(LX)</td><td>5) 比利时航空公司</td></tr>
<tr><td>(　　) f. emergency landing/ditching</td><td>6) 奥凯航空公司(中国)</td></tr>
<tr><td>(　　) g. life jacket</td><td>7) 瑞士航空公司</td></tr>
<tr><td>(　　) h. oxygen mask</td><td>8) 防冲撞</td></tr>
<tr><td>(　　) i. emergency evacuation</td><td>9) 港龙航空公司(中国香港)</td></tr>
<tr><td>(　　) j. brace against impact</td><td>10) 氧气面罩</td></tr>
</table>

2. Translate the following sentences into English.

1) 本架飞机共有八个安全出口，请找到离你最近的那个出口。

2) 由于飞机遇到强气流，请马上系上安全带。

3) 弯下身把您的头放在两膝之间，然后抱住双膝。

4) 请调直座椅靠背，固定好小桌板，收起脚踏板。

5) 请不要在机舱里将救生衣充气！一离开飞机立即拉下小红头充气。

6) 由于飞机遇到了强气流，所以洗手间暂时关闭。

7) 别担心，请保持安静，我们的机长有能力和信心安全着陆。

8) 我们的飞机可能得在备用机场过夜。

9) 由于飞机漏油需要紧急迫降。

10) 飞机完全停稳之前请您不要解开安全带。

3. Translate the following sentences into Chinese.

1) I'm sorry, Sir. I'm too nervous just now. I'm not quite clear. Would you show me that again?

2) Could you tell me something more about the weather at Shanghai Pudong International Airport.

3) Would you like to hold my son while I put my life vest on?

4) Excuse me, Miss. Can you refund the ticket for me if I do not want to take the plane?

5) The scheduled departure time has passed 20 minutes. What happened to the aircraft?

6) For your safety, please take away sharp objects such as earrings, watches, pens, high-heeled shoes and so on when you evacuate.

7) I will ask for my colleague to get an oxygen bottle for you as soon as possible!

8) Because of a mechanical trouble, the pressure in the cabin has reduced. Please pull the oxygen masks over your nose and mouth.

9) All our crew members are well trained for this kind of situation. Please obey our instructions carefully.

10) The most important duty of any crew member on board is to ensure the safety of the passengers all the time.

4. Suppose you are a flight attendant. Now the captain has decided to make an emergency landing. You are working as a flight attendant to help the passengers in the cabin. Please fill in the blanks of the following dialogue.

P：What happened，Miss?

FA：(1) _____.

P：My god! It's really terrible.

FA：(2) _____.

P：But could you show me how to put on my life vest again?

FA：(3) _____.

P：Oh，it's too nervous.

FA：(4) _____.

P：May I go to the toilet now?

FA：(5) _____.

5. Fill in the blanks in the following sentences with the words given below. Change the form where necessary.

| agency calmly scared comfort evacuate |
| leakage unfavorable competence rescue damage |

1) They all _____ when the enemy approached the city.

2) The government has _____ the company from bankruptcy by giving them a grant.

3) Drinking and smoking can _____ your health.

4) In spite of the _____ weather, the grain output of the farm kept up and even increased a little than last year.

5) The relief _____ distributed food among the poor.

6) We need a _____ leader to overcome these difficulties.

7) She replied to their angry question by _____ walking out of the room.

8) Large areas of land have been contaminated by the _____ from the nuclear reactor.

9) She _____ herself that her husband would be home soon.

10) Those who saw this horrifying punishment were always _____!

6. Complete the paragraph with the correct word in the box.

emergency	inflate	preparation	inform	upright
safety	remove	keep	instructions	captain

Ladies and Gentlemen:

Attention please! Our plane will soon make a/an 1) _____ landing/ditching due to the oil leakage from the aircraft and we can't continue any further. Don't be scared. Our 2) _____ has full confidence to land/ditch safely and all crew members will do our utmost to ensure your safety. We have contacted the Rescue Agency who will be waiting for us. We will 3) _____ you the time of landing/ditching later. So now we make personal 4) _____ for your safety on emergency landing/ditching. Please obey the 5) _____ of the flight attendants calmly. Firstly, return your seat to its 6) _____ position, stow all tray tables and straight up your footrest. Secondly, 7) _____ all sharp objects from your body to prevent injury such as jewelry, high-heeled shoes, pens, watches, necklace, earrings, eye glasses and so on. Put these objects in your carry-on baggage; For your 8) _____, put your hand luggage in the overhead compartment. Thirdly, put on your life vest but do not 9) _____ it until you have left the cabin. Finally, 10) _____ quiet and wait for further information from the flight attendants.

Thank you for your cooperation.

Section C　Supplementary Reading

Emergency Procedures

For as long as there have been aircrafts, there have been unexpected events that have emergency procedures in order to help ensure the safest possible outcome for both aircraft and crew. In aviation, emergencies are defined as situations in which immediate action by those involved is required in order to ensure the safety of a flight. In general, humans are ill equipped to deal consistently and effectively with emergencies.

A detailed set of guidelines or procedures for people to follow in the event of an emergency often helps to positively impact the emergency situation. These procedures have evolved from the relatively simple memorized procedures used by pilots of early aircraft to the relatively complex procedures used by a flight crew.

Emergency procedures range from small-aircraft checklists for dealing the accidental opening of a cabin door during flight to large commercial airports' detailed emergency plans for dealing with an incoming aircraft that has been rendered virtually uncontrollable.

Procedures in the Aircraft

In the case of a small aircraft, it is recommended that pilots carry a set of emergency procedures checklists readily available to them in the event of an emergency. These checklists may be in paper or electronic format. Emergency procedures cover a variety of topics dealing with engine failures, in-flight fires, electrical failures, flight control malfunctions and others.

Generally, the more complex the aircraft is, the more involved are the emergency procedures. In larger transport aircraft, more than one pilot is available to assist during crisis situations, and the delegation of responsibility at such times rests upon the pilot in command. In an emergency situation involving a multicrew aircraft, generally one pilot continues to fly and maintain control of the aircraft while the other pilot (or two) are freed up to focus on the emergency procedures.

Electronic Aids

In modern aircraft with electronic flight instrumentation there are often systems onboard the aircraft that will assist the flight crew in diagnosing a problem and will provide the appropriate checklist on what is called a multifunction display (MFD) on the flight deck. This display highlights the appropriate checklist items and forces the crew to acknowledge each checklist item before proceeding to the next item.

Larger aircraft, such as the Boeing 757 and 767, are equipped with an engine information and crew alerting system (EICAS), which immediately brings a fault diagnosis to the attention of the flight crew.

Cabin Safety

Emergency procedures also exist for the cabin crew, or flight attendants, and for passengers. All passengers are required by the Federal Aviation Regulations (FARs) to be briefed on these procedures by the cabin crew prior to flight. Research has shown that those passengers who listen to the preflight emergency briefing information are much more likely to survive an air accident than those who do not.

Airline cabin crew members are required to attend annual recurrent emergency procedures training. This training consists of a review of basic emergency and evacuation procedures for the particular aircraft the crew members fly.

Survival

In order to survive an air accident, the crew and passengers must be able to do three things successfully. First, they must survive the impact of the crash, if applicable. Second, they must evacuate the aircraft safely in a timely manner, especially in the event of a fire. Third, if the accident occurs away from an airport, they must survive the post-accident environmental conditions until they are rescued or until safety is reached. The first two items are often largely dependent upon how much attention was paid to the preflight safety briefing, whereas the third item depends upon previous training.

Airport Emergencies

The majority of aircraft accidents happen on the premises of an airport. If an aircraft accident occurs on or in the immediate vicinity of an airport, the occupants have a much greater chance of surviving the post-incident conditions, because all publicly certified airports have emergency action plans.

Every three years, certificated airports are required to conduct a live-fire training exercise under simulated accident conditions. In this exercise, the emergency action plan is put into effect, and all agencies react just as they would in an actual emergency. In this rehearsal, usually an aircraft is towed into a simulated crash position on the airport and costumed victims are situated in and around the aircraft, as they might be in an accident. Simulated crash victims are then extracted and treated, and fires are extinguished, allowing everyone involved a chance to identify areas of needed improvement in the plan.

A common theme throughout all aviation emergency procedures, whether they are on board an aircraft in flight or on the ground at an airport, is the importance of having structured, well-rehearsed and well-coordinated plans of action to follow. With these in place, human beings are much better able to perform under adverse circumstances, ensuring the minimum loss of life and damage to property.

Questions for discussion:

1. What do emergency procedures cover in the case of small aircraft?
2. How do pilots assist during crisis situations in larger transport aircraft?
3. How is each crew member aware of the checklist item and its completion status?
4. Who are much more likely to survive an air accident according to the research?
5. What exercises are certificated airports required to conduct every three years?

Section D   Interview English

Daily hot topic:

Family and friends

The typical questions on daily hot topic have been usually asked when you attend an interview. There are several examples. The answers are given for your reference.

1. Could you please say something about your family?

A: I'm from an extended family. There are five people in my family: my grandparents, my parents and I. My father is a doctor. My mother is a housewife. My father supports the family. I live in a harmonious family.

2. Do you have generation gap with your parents?

A: No. we haven't generation gap, especially with my mother. I like sharing my happiness and sadness with my mother. She is like my friend.

3. Do you like making friends?

A: Yes. I am an outgoing girl/boy. I don't like staying by myself. I am afraid of loneliness. Therefore, I like making friends very much. They can stay with me when I feel lonely.

4. How would your friends describe you?

A: They usually say I am warmhearted and friendly. They like staying with me because I am very humorous. They think staying with me is equal to staying with happiness.

5. What kind of people do you make friends with? why?

A: I make friends with honest people who don't lie to me because I am an honest boy/girl. They have to be my friend from the heart. My friends should be very smart on a critical moment. I think this kind of people can warn me against false decision.

Role-play practice:

You want to be a flight attendant and have an interview. The interviewer asks you what kind of friend is a true friend. Please make an interview role-play with your partner.

Unit 8

In-flight Entertainment

Lead-in questions

1. What could the passengers do on board if they feel bored?

2. What kinds of entertainment programs are usually offered during the flight?

3. What can you provide him if a passenger wants to have something to read?

Section A   Dialogues

Dialogue one

Setting: In the cabin, a passenger pushes the call button. A female flight attendant named Michael comes up to him.

(P: *passenger*)

Michael: Good morning, Sir. Can I help you?

P: Morning, Miss. May I have something to read?

Michael: Yes, we have some in-flight magazines and some newspapers. Which one would you like, Sir.

P: Em...what kind of papers do you have?

Michael: We have China Daily, People's Daily, New York Times, CAAC Journal, Readers' Digest and some local papers. Which would you prefer?

P: Please give me a copy of China Daily.

Michael: Wait a minute. Here you are.

P: Thank you. By the way, do you have CAAC in-flight magazine in English?

Michael: No. I'm sorry. Yet we have China Daily in English. Would you like to look through?

P: Ok, please give me a copy of China Daily in English.

Michael: Here you are.

P: Ok, now I am feeling a little cold. Would you help me turn off the cold air.

Michael: Of course, do you need a blanket?

P: No, I think I will feel better after you turn off the cold air. By the way, have you got anything to eat?

Michael: What do you think of some crackers, Sir.

P: I don't like eating crackers. Shall we have supper on board? I'm a little hungry.

Michael: I'm sorry, Sir. As this is a short flight, we only serve beverages and refreshments on board.

P: Ok. Thanks.

Dialogue two

Setting: The flight attendant called Michael is patrolling in the cabin. She finds that a lady is waving her hand. She comes up to her to give some help.

Michael: Excuse me. Do you need my help, Madam?

P1: Yes, I want to watch movies but I don't know how to use it.

Michael: Let me show you. Firstly, press the button on your armrest. Then select the Channel corresponding with the movie. After that, you can enjoy it.

P1: Oh, thank you. That's great. By the way, do you have any recommendations about the movie today.

Michael: What kind of movie would you like? Comedy, action, thriller, love story, tragedy or drama?

P1: Love story, please.

Michael: "Waterloo Bridge". Ok? It is an affecting story about love which tells a story between a dancer and an officer who met by chance on Waterloo Bridge.

P: It sounds very interesting. I like it. By the way, could you give me a pair of headsets?

Michael: Here you are, Madam.

P1: Thank you. Could you tell me how to use it?

Michael: Certainly, let me show you. First put the plugs into your ears. Then put this one into the jack at your armrest. After that, press the button to select the channel you want. Could you hear?

P1: Yeah. Thank you very much.

Michael: You are welcome.

(*At this time, another passenger has some problems.*)

P2: Excuse me, Miss. Could you give me a pair of headsets?

Michael: What's wrong with your headsets?

P2: One of the headsets doesn't work. Would you like to change it for me.

Michael: Yes, of course. Here you are.

P2: I want to listen to music. Could you help me adjust it?

Michael: Ok, there are several kinds of music, such as classical music, folk songs, pop music, light music and opera. Which would you like?

P2: I prefer opera. Which channel is it?

Michael: The fourth one. Have you got it?

P2: Yeah, I see. Thank you so much for everything you've done for me. It has been a comfortable flight.

Michael: I'm very glad you enjoy the flight. Have a good trip!

Words and expressions

journal /ˈdʒɜːnl/	n.	杂志,期刊
digest /daiˈdʒest/	n.	摘要,文摘
cracker /ˈkrækə/	n.	薄脆饼干
patrol /pəˈtrəul/	v.	巡逻;巡查
channel /ˈtʃænl/	n.	频道
correspond /ˌkɔrisˈpɔnd/	v.	相符合,相一致
recommendation /ˌrekəmenˈdeiʃən/	n.	推荐,建议
comedy /ˈkɔmidi/	n.	喜剧
thriller /ˈθrilə/	n.	(电影)惊悚片
tragedy /ˈtrædʒidi/	n.	悲剧,惨剧
drama /ˈdrɑːmə/	n.	戏剧
jack /dʒæk/	n.	插座
headsets /ˈhedsets/	n.	戴在头上的耳机或听筒
classical /ˈklæsikəl/	a.	古典的
folk /fəuk/	a.	民间的,民俗
pop /pɔp/	a.	流行音乐的,通俗的

opera /'ɔpərə/　　　　　　　　　　　　*n.* 歌剧

Exercises

1. Questions for discussion.

1) How do you help a passenger if he doesn't know how to use the earphones?

2) How do you help her if a young girl feels bored on board?

3) What do you offer for children if they are not interested in the programs provided on board?

4) What should you do if a passenger doesn't know how to use the entertainment system?

5) How do you help the passengers to select the movie?

2. Oral Practice.

Work with a partner to make up dialogues. Situational settings are as follows:

1) A passenger is complaining to you that the headsets do not work well. He/she wants to listen to music or watch movie, but he/she doesn't know how to adjust it. You'd better help him/her.

2) A passenger says that he feels bored on board, and ask how to entertain himself.

Section B　Announcements

Announcement(I)

Good morning, ladies and gentlemen,

May I have your attention, please? Now we have reached our cruising altitude. In order to enrich your life on board, the in-flight entertainment will begin. We hope you will enjoy it.

Please put on your headsets and select the channel which corresponds with the program that you wish to watch. If you have any questions, please call your flight attendant for assistance. Thank you!

Announcement (II)

Ladies and Gentlemen,

We are pleased to offer you in-flight entertainment program shortly. We hope you will enjoy it.

Headsets will be available from your flight attendants. If you have any questions, please tell us. Thank you!

Announcement (III)

Ladies and Gentlemen,

We regret to inform you that the video system is not available on this flight. Only audio programs can be accessed. Headsets may be obtained from your flight attendants. If you need any assistance, please don't hesitate to contact us. Thank you.

Words and expressions

enrich /inˈritʃ/	v.	充实，使丰富
assistance /əˈsistəns/	n.	帮助，援助，支持
access /ækses/	vt.	使用；接近

Exercises

1. Match the English phrases in column A with the Chinese translations in column B.

A	B
( ) a. Yunnan Airlines (3Q)	1）四川航空公司
( ) b. United Airlines (UA)	2）民乐
( ) c. Asiana Airlines (OZ)	3）京剧
( ) d. Sichuan Airlines (3U)	4）纽约时报
( ) e. Qantas Airways (QF)	5）美国联合航空公司
( ) f. classical music	6）中国日报
( ) g. folk song	7）云南航空公司
( ) h. Peking opera	8）澳洲航空公司
( ) i. China Daily	9）古典音乐
( ) j. New York Times	10）韩亚航空公司

2. Translate the following sentences into English.

1）您想翻看报纸或杂志吗？

2）我们有《中国日报》《财经时代》《中国民航》《纽约时报》和一些地方报纸。您想看哪种？

3）我们将播放电影、流行音乐、民乐、古典音乐和京剧。

4）很抱歉机上视频系统发生故障，但是我们有大量的音频节目供您选择。

5）飞机马上就要到达伦敦国际机场，我们的娱乐节目即将结束。

6）你能给我几份英文报纸或杂志吗？我想翻阅一下。

7）对于头等舱和商务舱的旅客，电视机就在您的手扶里。

8）女士，打扰一下，您能告诉我现在放映的是什么电影吗？

9）请按手扶上的按钮来选择您喜欢的频道。

10）顺便问一下，今天你有什么好电影推荐吗？

3. Translate the following sentences into Chinese.

1）Excuse me, Sir. I don't know how to use the headsets. Can you show me how to use them?

2）Excuse me, Miss. One of the headsets doesn't work. Could you please change it for me?

3) Excuse me. I want to read something. Have you got any English newspaper or magazines?

4) Can you help me adjust it? I want to see a film.

5) Miss, could you give me any recommendations about the movie today?

6) Earphones may be obtained from the flight attendants free of charge on this flight.

7) Please select the channel that corresponds with the movie you are watching or the music you want to listen to.

8) I like this pair of headsets very much. May I take it home?

9) The headsets are in the seat pocket in front of you. If you want to watch movies or listen to music, you may use them.

10) We do apologize that the TV set isn't operating properly. I will check if there is another seat available for you to move to.

4. Suppose you are a flight attendant. Now a woman with a little boy asks for your help. She asks if there are any entertainments for children on board. You are working as a flight attendant to help the passengers in the cabin. Please fill in the blanks of the following dialogue according to your understanding.

P: Excuse me, Miss. Are there any entertainments for my son?

FA: (1) _____.

P: How considerate of you!

FA: (2) _____.

P: My son wants to watch animated movies. Would you like to help me adjust it?

FA: (3) _____.

P: Could you give me any advice for my son?

FA: (4) _____.

P: Yeah, he likes watching it very much.

FA: (5) _____.

5. Fill in the blanks in the following sentences with the words given below. Change the form where necessary.

enrich   recommendation   assistance   present   acquire
encounter   comedy   correspond   digest   classical

1) Does he prefer _____ or tragedy?

2) The copy doesn't _____ with the original.

3) Did you _____ anyone in the building?

4) My father is very interested in _____ architecture.

5) Everyone should _____ the mind with knowledge.

6) You should _____ what your boss said at meeting.

7) The company has recently _____ new offices in central London.

8) The government has agreed to implement the _____ in the report.

9) The problem naturally _____ itself in my mind.

10) You can not rely on your parents' _____ all the times.

6. Complete the paragraph with the correct word in the box.

> show　charge　hesitate　enjoy　choice
> requirement　corresponds　watching　acquired　listen

Good morning, ladies and gentlemen,

　　We are going to 1) _____ the film "Jurassic Park" shortly. There is also a 2) _____ of folk songs, classical music, light music, and Beijing opera. Headsets may be 3) _____ from the flight attendants free of 4) _____ on this flight. Please select the channel that 5) _____ with the movie you are 6) _____ or the music you want to 7) _____ . If you have any 8) _____ , please don't 9) _____ to ask the cabin attendants. We hope you 10) _____ the rest of the flight.

　　Thank you.

Section C　Supplementary Reading

Varieties of In-flight Entertainment

Moving-map systems

A moving-map system is a real-time flight information video channel broadcast through to cabin video screens and personal televisions (PTVs). In addition to displaying a map that illustrates the position and direction of the plane, the system gives the altitude, airspeed, outside air temperature, distance to the destination, distance from the origination point, and local time. The moving-map system information is derived in real time from the aircraft's flight computer systems.

Audio entertainment

Audio entertainment covers music, as well as news, information, and comedy. Most music channels are pre-recorded and feature their own DJs to provide chatter, song introductions, and interviews with artists. In addition, there is sometimes a channel devoted to the plane's radio communications, allowing passengers to listen in on the pilot's in-flight conversations with other planes and ground stations.

In audio-video on demand (AVOD) systems, entertainment is experienced through headphones that are distributed to the passengers. The headphone plugs are usually only compatible with the audio socket on the passenger's armrest (and vice versa) , and some airlines may charge a small fee to obtain a pair. The headphones provided can also be used for the viewing of personal televisions.

Video entertainment

Video entertainment is provided via a large video screen at the front of a cabin section, as well as smaller monitors situated every few rows above the aisles. Sound is supplied via the same headphones as those distributed for audio entertainment.

However, personal televisions (PTVs) for every passenger provide passengers with channels broadcasting new and classic films, as well as comedies, news, sports programming, documentaries, children's shows, and drama series. Some airlines also present news and current affairs programming, which are often pre-recorded and delivered in the early morning before flights commence.

PTVs are operated via an In flight Management System which stores pre-recorded channels on a central server and streams them to PTV equipped seats during flight. AVOD systems store individual programs separately, allowing a passenger to have a specific program streamed to them privately, and be able to control the playback.

Some airlines also provide video games as part of the video entertainment system. For example, Singapore Airlinespassengers on some flights have access to a number of Super Nintendo games as part of its *KrisWorld* entertainment system. Also Virgin America's and V Australia's new *RED* Entertainment System offers passengers internet gaming over a Linux-basedoperating system.

Personal televisions

Some airlines have now installed personal televisions (otherwise known as PTVs) for every passenger on most long-haul routes. These televisions are usually located in the seat-backs or tucked away in the armrests for front row seats and first class. Some show direct broadcast satellite television which enables passengers to view live TV broadcasts. Some airlines also offer video games using PTV equipment. Fewer still provide closed captioning for deaf and hard-of-hearing passengers.

Audio-video on demand (AVOD) entertainment has also been introduced. This enables passengers to pause, rewind, fast-forward, or stop a program that they have been watching. This is in contrast to older entertainment systems where no interactivity is provided for. AVOD also allows the passengers to choose among movies stored in the aircraft computer system.

In-flight movies

Personal on-demand videos are stored in an aircraft's main in-flight entertainment system, from whence they can be viewed on demand by a passenger over the aircraft's built in media server and wireless broadcast system. Along with the on-demand concept comes the ability for the user to pause, rewind, fast forward, or jump to any point in the movie. There are also movies that are shown throughout the aircraft at one time, often on shared overhead screens or a screen in the front of the cabin. More modern aircraft are now allowing Personal Electronic Devices (PED's) to be used to connect to the on board in-flight entertainment systems.

Regularly scheduled in flight movies began to premiere in 1961 on flights from New York to Los Angeles.

Closed-captioning

Closed-captioning technology for deaf and hard-of-hearing passengers started in 2008 with Emirates Airlines. The captions are text streamed along with video and spoken audio and enables passengers to either enable or disable the subtitle/caption language. Closed captioning is capable of streaming various text languages, including Arabic, Chinese, English, French, German, Hindi, Spanish, and Russian.

Questions for discussion.

1. What can moving-map systems display?

2. What are the headphone plugs usually only compatible with?

3. What do personal televisions (PTVs) provide for every passenger?

4. What does (AVOD) entertainment enable passengers to do?

5. When is closed captioning technology started?

Section D　Interview English

Daily hot topic:

Cabin service

The typical questions on daily hot topic have been usually asked when you attend an interview. There are several examples. The answers are given for your reference.

1. How would you do if you were a flight attendant?

A: I would be friendly and warm-hearted to every passenger. I would try to provide them with comfortable service such as at home.

2. If you have a passenger who insults you, what would you do?

A: I'll tell him/her please pay attention to the words you speak. We should respect each other. At the same time I won't spend time getting into a discussion with him.

3. If a passenger takes a wrong seat, how do you deal with? What would you say to him/her?

A: Excuse me, Ms/Sir. May I see your boarding card? I'm afraid you are in the wrong seat. Your seat number is 35B, yet you are sitting at 25B now. Would you like to your seat 35B?

4. Have you realized that being a flight attendant is a vey hard job? Could you overcome the difficulties met at work?

A: Yea, I'm fully aware of that. Since I choose this career, I believe I have the confidence and competence to overcome all kinds of difficulties met at work.

5. If a passenger flirts with you and wants to know your phone number. What would you do?

A: Firmly but politely tell him we aren't permitted to tell our private phone numbers to passengers, which is our airlines' regulation. I hope you can understand. Thank you for your cooperation.

Role-play practice:

You want to be a flight attendant and have an interview. The interviewer asks you if a passenger isn't satisfied with your service, he complains to your chief purser. What will you do? Please make an interview role-play with your partner.

Unit 9
Duty Free Sales

Lead-in questions

1. Do you usually like to buy some duty-free goods during the flight?

2. Do you know what kinds of duty-free goods are usually sold on board?

3. What kinds of duty-free goods will you suggest if a passenger asks for your advice?

Section A   Dialogues

Dialogue one

Setting：A flight attendant named Della is serving the passengers，and a gentleman is choosing something beside the cart.

（P：Passenger）

Della：What can I do for you?

P：I want to buy something for myself.

Della：What would you like to buy?

P：I have no idea. Could you give me some advice?

Della：Certainly. We have a wide selection of fragrances，skin-care products，cosmetics，sunglasses，jewelry，watches，leather goods，cigars and some liquor，chocolate candies，children's toys，popular digital products and so on.

P：I'd like to buy some liquor. What kinds of liquor do you have，Miss?

Della：We have Glenfiddich，Chivas Regal，Johnnie Walker Red Label，Johnnie Walker Black Label，Rye Whisky，Dynasty，and Brandy. Which one would you like?

P：Both my father and I like to drink Whisky. Thus I decide to buy a bottle of Chivas Regal and a bottle of Johnnie Walker Black Label. One is for me，the other is for my father.

Della:Ok,wait a moment,please. Here you are.

P:How much should I pay you altogether?

Della:It comes to $58.00,Sir.

P:Can I have a discount?

Della:I'm sorry. All the items provided on board are at marked prices.

P:May I use credit card?

Della:Sure,Sir.

P:Here is my card.

Della:Thank you. Please input your cipher.

P:Ok.

Della:Please sign your name here.

P:Yeah. It is very nice of you to do all that for me.

Della:We are looking forward to serving you again some day.

Dialogue two

Setting:A flight attendant named Della is patrolling with a cart along the aisle,on top of which an attractive display of items is arranged. A woman is waving her hand.

P:Excuse me,Miss. Do you sell duty-free items in the cabin?

Della:Yes,we will offer duty-free items in a while.

P:Do you have duty-free cosmetics on board?

Della:Certainly, Here is the Duty-free Guide. Firstly,you may look it through. Then please tell me what you want.

P:Ok. But would you give me some advice?

Della:Sure. We have perfume,lip stick,eye shadow/cream,face cream,skin milk and so on.

P:I want to buy a bottle of face cream. Which brand is better?

Della:I think Lancome is ok. I like using it.

P:Is it expensive?

Della:It's 46 US dollars.

P:Ok,would you like to get it for me?

Della:Certainly. By the way,would you like to buy something else?

P:Yeah,I nearly forget. My daughter asks me to buy a doll for her.

Della:I'm sorry, Madam. That has been sold out. This one is very popular today because tomorrow is Children's Day.

P:Could you recommend something for my daughter?

Della:How old is she?

P:She is twelve years old.

Della: How about all kinds of accessories?

P: Yeah, my daughter likes these things very much. Have you got anything brighter? Something more Chinese?

Della: Sure. What about the silk scarves? It's a conventional design and the colors are bright.

Della: Yeah, very nice. Is it pure silk?

P: Of course, pure silk.

P: This is very beautiful. How much is it?

Della: It's 25 US dollars.

P: I will take it plus tax?

Della: All the items sold on board are duty free.

P: Would you accept traveler's check?

Della: Sorry, Madam. You need to pay in cash.

P: Ok, how much are they together?

Della: Let me see, face cream is 46 US dollars and the silk scarf is 25 US dollars. That comes to 71 US dollars.

P: It is 100 US dollars.

Della: Here's your change, 29 US dollars.

P: You've been most helpful.

Della: It's our duty to do this.

Words and Expressions

duty-free		免税的
selection /si'lekʃən/	n.	可供选择的东西
fragrance /'freigrəns/	n.	香水
sunglasses /'sʌnˌglæsiz/	n.	太阳眼镜
tie /tai/	n.	领带
cigar /si'gɑ:/	n.	雪茄烟
liquor /'likə/	n.	烈性酒
Glenfiddich		格兰菲迪(纯麦威士忌)
rye /raɪ/	n.	黑麦
Brandy /'brændi/	n.	白兰地酒
discount /'diskaunt/	n.	折扣
item /'aɪtəm/	n.	条款，一件商品(或物品)
credit card		信用卡
cipher /'saifə/	n.	密码
attractive /ə'træktiv/	a	有吸引力的

display /dis'plei/	n.	陈列,展览
cosmetic /kɔz'metik/	n.	化妆品
perfume /'pəːfjuːm/	n.	香水
lip stick		口红
eye shadow		眼影膏
brand /brænd/	n.	商标,牌子
Lancome		(法国化妆品牌)兰蔻
doll /dɔl/	n.	(玩具)娃娃
accessory /æk'sesəri/	n.	妇女饰品
scarf /skɑːf/	n.	围巾
conventional /kən'venʃ(ə)n(ə)l/	a	传统的
tax /tæks/	n.	税,税额
check /tʃek/	n.	支票
cash /kæʃ/	n.	现金
change /tʃeindʒ/	n.	零钱

Exercises

1. Questions for discussion.

1) How do you explain when a passenger wants to buy many bottles of Maotai on board?

2) What should you say to a passenger when he wants to buy silk scarves which you don't carry on board?

3) How do you explain to the passenger when a passenger would like to buy a bottle of Lancome face cream but it was sold out?

4) What should you say to a passenger if she bargains with you while you sell duty-free goods?

5）A passenger wants to pay in check for duty-free goods，but you don't accept it. What would you explain to him?

2. Oral Practice.

Work with a partner to make up dialogues. Situational settings are as follows.

1) The plane has entered the cruising altitude. Now duty-free sales begin. After you give a brief introduction to all the items on board，a passenger asks for your recommendation because she wants to buy some gifts for her family.

2）A passenger wants to buy five bottles of Whiskey，which has exceeded the limit. She decides to buy two bottles after you tell her the limitation on duty-free liquor. He also asks for some discount，which is not allowed on board.

Section B　Announcements

Announcements（I）

Ladies and Gentlemen，

Good afternoon! In order to further meet your traveling needs，we will provide you many local products and international brands. You can select your goods from the duty-free magazine in the seat pocket in front of you. Your cabin attendant is pleased to assist you. All prices are shown in US dollars. Please check with your cabin attendant for prices in other currencies. Most currencies and US dollars，traveler's checks，the major credit cards are accepted for your purchases. Have a good trip!

Thank you.

Announcements（II）

Ladies and Gentlemen，

We will begin our in-flight Duty-free sales service shortly. Our duty-free Goods Catalog，with product information，can be found in the seat pocket in front of you. For your convenience，we accept both cash and major international credit cards.

For transit passengers，please note that liquid items purchased onboard are subject to Safety Regulations on Prohibiting Liquid Items onboard. Please feel free to contact any of our flight attendants for more information.

Thank you very much!

Words and Expressions

exclusive /iks'kluːsiv/	a.	高级的，奢华的	
currency /'kʌrənsi/	n.	货币	
purchase /'pəːtʃəs/	n.	购买，买到的东西	
description /dis'kripʃn/	n.	描述，说明	
catalog /'kætələg/	n.	目录	
liquid /'likwid/	a.	液体的	
prohibit /prə'hibit/	v.	禁止，阻止	

Exercises

1. Match the English phrases in column A with the Chinese translations in column B.

A	B
（　　） a. Iran Air (IR)	1）美国西南航空公司
（　　） b. duty free items	2）口红

( ) c. Vietnam Airlines（VN）   3）埃及航空公司

( ) d. direct flight   4）伊朗航空公司

( ) e. Air Egypt（MS）   5）转机

( ) f. Philippine Airlines（PR）   6）免税品

( ) g. eye shadow   7）菲律宾航空公司

( ) h. Southwest Airlines（WN）   8）直机

( ) i. lip stick   9）越南航空公司

( ) j. connecting flight   10）眼影

2. Translate the following sentences into English.

1）为了满足您的旅行需求，我们将在飞机上为您提供各种免税品。

2）如果您想了解其他货币标价，请咨询乘务员。

3）您有很多种选择，例如糖果、玩具、卡通书等。

4）很抱歉，飞机上供应的商品都是明码标价的。

5）很抱歉我们不接收支票，你只能付现金或用信用卡。

6）打扰一下女士，请问飞机上卖免税品吗？

7）先生您好，请问您想买点什么免税品？

8）这个化妆品太贵了，你能给我点折扣吗？

9）免税品宣传册就在您前面的座椅口袋里，您可以先浏览一下。

10）机上所有的免税品都是以美元标价。

3. Translate the following sentences into Chinese.

1）What's the exchange rate between US dollar and RMB?

2）Could you recommend something as a gift for my son?

3）I've heard so much about the famous Remy Martin X. O. and I've been wanting to taste it for a long time.

4）I heard that China is famous for silk. That's just what I need. Could you give me some suggestions?

5）I'm afraid the color isn't suitable for my wife. Do you have a pink one?

6）We don't accept tips. It's our duty to serve you well.

7）I haven't got enough change for you, Madam. Please wait for a minute. I will be back soon.

8）Could you tell me how many bottles of alcohol I can take to China?

9）I'd like to buy some whisky for my father as presents. What kind of whisky do you have on board, Sir?

10）May I know what currencies I can use to purchase the duty-free goods?

4. Suppose you are a flight attendant. A gentleman wants to know what kind of duty free goods you have on board. He asks you to recommend something as a gift for his wife.

P：Excuse me, Miss?

FA：(1) _____ .

P:Yes,I want to buy something as a birthday present for my wife. Would you give me some advice?

FA:(2)_____.

P:So many choices! Which one is better?

FA:(3)_____.

P:Oh,very nice. How much is it?

FA:(4)_____.

P:May I use traveler's check?

FA:(5)_____.

5. Fill in the blanks in the following sentences with the words given below. Change the form where necessary.

> exclusive display discount attractive cipher
> description currency check change purchase

1) Would you tell me something about foreign _____ accounts?

2) Can you give us an accurate _____ of the goods?

3) The _____ price is less if you pay cash.

4) Can I pay by _____ or credit card?

5) That movie star often goes to the _____ restaurants.

6) Will you _____ me five ten-pound notes?

7) The bigger _____ attracted more customers but very few of them actually bought the new products.

8) The advantages of our products are _____ design, high quality and reasonable prices.

9) The government uses a special _____ so that official messages are kept secret.

10) We offer you 25% _____ for group reservation.

6. Complete the paragraph with the correct word in the box.

> conclude purchase discover contact begin
> available board currencies accepted brands

Ladies and Gentlemen,

Good morning! Duty-free sales will 1) _____ in a moment. Product descriptions are 2) _____ in the Duty-free Catalog, which is in the seat pocket. Within the Duty-free Catalog you may 3) _____ all kinds of items from the world's most popular 4) _____, such as cosmetics from Chanel, Lancome, SK-II; jewelry from Cartier, Tiffany, Prada; liquor from Whisky, Vodka, bags from Louis Vuitton, Hermes, Tod's; watches from Breguet, Piaget Rolex; tobacco from Warboro, Salem, Camel. All the goods sold on 5) _____ are tax free. If you would like to 6) _____, please 7) _____ with your flight attendant. Most major 8)

_____ and US dollars, traveler's checks are 9) _____ for your purchases. Duty-free sales will 10) _____ twenty minutes before landing.

Thank you!

Section C   Supplementary Reading

American Airlines Discontinues Duty-Free Sales on International Flights

American Airlines ended all in-flight sales of duty-free items late last week. The Fort Worth-based airline said that the move came following a dispute with its vendor.

"American Airlines has stopped selling duty free merchandise on select international flights as of Friday, March 20, 2015, due to a contractual disagreement between American Airlines and DFASS, the company that had handled our onboard duty free sales". the airline told Frequent Business Traveler.

The carrier is currently in the process of removing duty-free items, catalogs, and ads from its planes. Sales of duty-free items on some US Airways international flights "will continue" until further notice, the airline said.

However, American is not the first major U. S. airline to discontinue duty-free sales. Delta Air Lines ended in-flight sales last August following a dispute with the airline's duty-free vendor.

At the time Delta dropped its duty-free operations, a Delta purser, who asked that his name not be used as he was not authorized to speak on behalf of the airline, told Frequent Business Traveler he was "happy" to hear the news. He explained that he felt the change would improve the in-flight experience for passengers, who considered it more of a disruption than a benefit.

With the increase in duty-free stores at airports as well as the greater availability of goods on the Internet, duty-free in-flight sales have been declining over the past decades.

While on-board sales have been discontinued, virtually all international airports offer duty-free shops where travelers can make purchases. Duty-free shopping can be traced back to the 1940s when Brendan O'Regan opened up a duty-free shop that sold Irish goods to passengers on a refueling stop at Rineanna (now Shannon) Airport where he served as catering controller.

Questions for discussion.

1. Why did the American Airlines stop selling duty free goods?

2. Why was the frequent business traveler happy at the news that Delta dropped its

duty-free operations?

3. What has happened to duty-free in-flight sales over the past decades? What's the reason for that?

4. When can duty-free shopping be traced back to?

5. How did a Delta purser feel the change on duty-free operations?

Section D   Interview English

Daily hot topic：

Interpersonal relationship

The typical questions on daily hot topic have been usually asked when you attend an interview. There are several examples. The answers are given for your reference.

1. Do you think how to maintain good relationship with your colleagues?

A：I think first we should respect others, as an old saying goes；if you want others to respect you, you need respect others first. Second, we shouldn't be selfish. If we are selfish we can not make a true friend. At last we should communicate with our colleagues well.

2. How would you deal with the trouble met at work?

A：I would do my upmost to handle it, and if I couldn't solve it, I would ask my colleagues to assist me.

3. What kind of colleagues do you want to work with?

A：I'd like to work with colleagues who are honest, responsible and hardworking.

4. What kind of boss do you want to work for?

A：I'd like to work for boss who's efficient but strict because I strongly dislike inefficiency. I think it's completely reasonable for a boss to be strict.

5. What have you learned about dealing with people from your experience?

A：I've learned that listening is the most important part of dealing with people. You have to put yourself into others' shoes. It is also important to treat everyone with respect because every person at every level wants to be respected.

Role-play practice：

You want to be a flight attendant and have an interview. The interviewer asks you whether you have any personal philosophies about working with people. Please make an interview role-play with your partner.

Unit 10

Transfer Service

Lead-in questions

1. How should a passenger deal with her carry-on luggage when disembarking if she continues her journey on the same flight?

2. A passenger doesn't know how to go through the transfer formalities to Shenyang. How do you help him?

3. How do you comfort a passenger who is worried about her connecting flight because her flight can't arrive on schedule?

Section A   Dialogues

Dialogue one

Setting: In the cabin, Jack pressed the call button, and he asked a female flight attendant for his connecting flight.

(P: Passenger)

FA: Excuse me, Sir. Is there anything I can do for you?

Jack:Yeah,would you spare me a minute,Miss? I've got a question.

FA:Of course.

Jack:Well,it seems that we will be late for Hong Kong International Airport.

FA:Yes, I'm afraid so. There is a heavy thunderstorm ahead of us. We have to fly around the thunderstorm and we expect to arrive at Hong Kong International Airport twenty minutes behind schedule.

Jack:Wow,twenty minutes? I'm afraid I'll miss my connecting flight to Shenyang.

FA:I'm sorry for delaying. May I know your departure time of your connecting flight?

Jack:Umm,it's 3:50 p. m. ,while we'll arrive at Hong Kong International Airport at 3:20 p. m. ,so there are only thirty minutes left.

FA:Don't worry, Sir. If you miss the flight,you may go to the ticket counter and they'll make a new arrangement for you.

Jack:Could you tell me where the ticket counter is? I don't know how to do with the following procedure.

FA:Ok,could you show me your passport? I would check it for you.

Jack:Here you are.

FA:You'll have to go to the domestic terminal after you get down. It's just beside the international terminal. You should reconfirm your reservation at the domestic transfer booking office.

Jack:Need I claim and transfer my baggage?

FA:I'm afraid so. Sorry for having brought you inconvenience.

Jack:I see. By the way,may I use my mobile phone? I want to tell my girl friend that the aircraft is delayed. Because she is meeting me there,We have planned to go to Shenyang together.

FA:I am sorry to say that your mobile phone can't be used on board at any time.

Jack:Ok. Thank you.

FA:You're welcome.

Dialogue two

Setting:Jack has landed at Hong Kong International Airport,and he is late for his connecting flight to Shenyang due to the delay of Flight MU1311. He has to go to the Flight Connections Center to make a new transit.An airport clerk called Shirley helps him.

Jack:Excuse me,Miss. I missed my connecting flight to Shenyang. May I make a new transit to Shenyang?

Shirley:Yes,of course. I'm sorry to hear that. We will make alternate arrangements for you.

Jack:It's ok. What time is the flight from Hong Kong to Shenyang? I want to get to

Shenyang as early as possible because my girl friend is flying there. I hope to see her at the airport earlier.

Shirley: Let me check it for you. You can take CZ2228 which leaves Hong Kong at 4:30 p.m.

Jack: Is it a direct flight or connecting flight?

Shirley: Connecting flight, you have to transit in Beijing.

Jack: Do you have direct flights today?

Shirley: Yes, but the departure time is at 7:50 p.m. It arrives in Shenyang at 00:20 a.m. next morning.

Jack: Oh, it's a little late. I prefer the connecting flight. Please book that flight for me.

Shirley: Ok, Here you are. I do apologize for any inconvenience caused by this delay and try our best to provide safety and comfort for you.

Jack: Well, could you tell me where I should go then?

Shirley: Oh, let me have a look, your boarding gate is No. 33. You need to follow the "connections" sign from Gate 30 to Gate 35, walk straight until you get to Gate 33.

Jack: I see, many thanks.

Shirley: It's my pleasure.

(*Now the time is 4:45 p.m. Jack is sitting on board. The aircraft hasn't taken off yet. Jack asks a flight attendant the reasons.*)

Jack: Excuse me, Miss. Now it's 4:45 p.m. Why hasn't our aircraft taken off yet? It is already 15 minutes past the scheduled departure time. What's wrong with the aircraft?

FA: There is nothing wrong with the plane. We are waiting for the plane in front of us to take off.

Jack: Oh. My God! How long do we have to wait?

FA: We have checked with the ground staff. They told us to take off at 4:50 p.m. . So we'll be able to take off at once.

Jack: Um, I have a connecting flight in Beijing. The departure delay will affect my next flight.

FA: I hope we will arrive at the destination on schedule. We will do our utmost to make your connecting formalities smooth and timely.

Jack: I hope so, too. Thank you.

FA: My pleasure. Have a good trip.

Words and Expressions

disembark /ˌdisimˈbɑːk/	v.	（使）登陆(上岸)
transfer /trænsˈfəː/	v.	（使在旅途中）转乘，换乘，倒车
spare /spɛə/	v.	抽出，分出，腾出
passport /ˈpɑːspɔːt/	n.	护照

domestic /dəˈmestik/	a.	本国的,国内的
terminal /ˈtəːmɪn(ə)l/	n.	终点站
reconfirm /ˌriːkənˈfəːm/	v.	重新确认
reservation /ˌrezəˈveiʃən/	n.	预订;预订的房间(或火车票、飞机票等)
claim /kleim/	v.	索取,认领
Flight Connection Center		转机中心
clerk /klɑːk/	n.	职员
direct flight		直航
boarding gate		登机口
destination /ˌdestiˈneiʃən/	n.	目的地,终点

Exercises

1. Questions for discussion.

1) How do you assist a foreign passenger who doesn't know how to go through the transfer formalities to Shanghai?

2) How do you explain to a passenger who doesn't know where the transit counter is at the airport?

3) How can a passenger find the flight connection center in the terminal building?

4) What suggestions do you give to a transit passenger if she is late for her transit flight?

5) What will you say if you can't give a definite answer to a passenger's question about transferring formalities?

2. Oral Practice.

Work with a partner to make up dialogues. Situational settings are as follows.

1) This is a flight from Seattle to Beijing. A passenger has a connecting flight from Beijing to Xi'an. He asks you for some information about transferring procedures after arriving in Beijing.

2) The flight cannot arrive at the destination airport on time due to heavy fog there. A passenger is worried about his connecting flight from Shanghai to Kunming. You tell him the ground staff will help her with the transit formalities.

Section B　Announcements

Announcements（I）

Ladies and Gentlemen,

Our plane will be landing immediately. The temperature outside is _____ degrees Celsius (or _____ degrees Fahrenheit.)

Please keep seated until our aircraft stops completely. Please caution when retrieving items from the overhead compartments.

Passengers, please take all your belongings when you disembark. Your checked baggage may be claimed in the baggage claim area.

Passengers, if you first enter the country, please take your passports and all your belongings to complete your entry formalities in the terminal building. Your checked baggage may be claimed in the baggage claim hall.

Passengers continuing to _____, attention please! The aircraft will stay here for about _____ minutes. When you disembark, please obtain your transit card from the ground staff, and complete the quarantine and immigration procedures in the terminal. Customs formality will be finished at _____ Airport (destination).

There will be a crew change here. Thank you for flying with us. Have a good trip!

Announcements（II）

Ladies and Gentlemen,

Attention, please. We're sorry to inform you that _____ airport has been closed due to a heavy thunderstorm there. Thus we have to divert to _____ International Airport. We'll land at _____ International Airport in 15 minutes. Then we will make a new arrangement for you to _____ as quickly as we can. If you have any connecting flights to other cities, please contact our flight attendants. We will assist you with the transfer after landing. We are awfully sorry for the inconvenience and appreciate your understanding.

Words and Expressions

degrees celsius /ˈselsɪəs/		摄氏度
Fahrenheit /ˈfær(ə)nhait/	*n.*	华氏温度
retrieve /riˈtriːv/	*v.*	取回
checked baggage		托运的行李
baggage claim area		行李认领处
obtain /əbˈtein/	*v.*	获得，得到
quarantine /ˈkwɒrəntiːn/	*n.*	检疫
immigration /ˌimiˈgreiʃən/	*n.*	（机场、港口等）移民局检查站
customs /ˈkʌstəmz/	*n.*	海关

Exercises

1. Match the English phrases in column A with the Chinese translations in column B.

A	B
(　　) a. All Nippon Airways(NH)	1) 登机口

(   ) b. Air Koryo（JS）   2）转机中心

(   ) c. Varig Brazilian Airlines（RG）   3）全日本航空公司

(   ) d. Malaysian Airlines（MH）   4）转机手续

(   ) e. Pakistan International Airlines（PK）   5）托运的行李

(   ) f. checked baggage   6）朝鲜航空公司

(   ) g. baggage claim hall   7）巴基斯坦国际航空公司

(   ) h. Flight Connection Center   8）巴西航空公司

(   ) i. boarding gate   9）马来西亚航空公司

(   ) j. transferring formalities   10）行李认领大厅

2. Translate the following sentences into English.

1）请抓紧时间。您转乘的班机还有三十分钟就要起飞了。

2）本架飞机会在重庆经停。整个航程需要大约 5 个小时。

3）乘客安检时应该准备好机票和身份证。

4）我能知道你的转乘班机的起飞时间吗?

5）您可以将行李留在飞机上,但贵重物品须随身携带。

6）先生您好,我是您的礼宾专员,我会带您到登机口。

7）本次航班延误了,恐怕我要错过去上海的转机。

8）很抱歉给您带来的不便,由于暴风雨,上海虹桥国际机场关闭,我们只能改落杭州国际机场。

9）别担心,我们会为您提供免费的食宿,并且会尽快安排您飞往纽约。

10）如果您还要中转航班的话,必须在报关后去国内候机厅等候。

3. Translate the following sentences into Chinese.

1）Could you tell me how long we'll stay at the alternate airport?

2）Why hasn't our plane taken off yet? It is already 20 minutes past the scheduled departure time.

3）How long do we have to wait? I have a connecting flight in Beijing. The departure delay will affect my next flight.

4）Why are we going to land at Guangzhou Baiyun Airport? Our destination is Shenzhen International Airport.

5）I want to buy an open-ticket to New York as I'm not sure when I will return.

6）You may go to the domestic terminal after you disembark. It's beside the international terminal.

7）Excuse me, Sir. You have some time before boarding. Would you like to have a rest in the refreshment lounge?

8）You can enter the terminal building by boarding bridge or ferry bus after deplaning from this flight.

9）You'd better check with the transfer counter in the arrival hall. They will be able to assist you.

10) If you are continuing your journey with us, your carry-on luggage may be left on board, but take your valuables and important documents with you.

4. Suppose you are a flight attendant. A foreign passenger doesn't know how to go through the transit formalities to Kunming. She asks for your help.

P: Excuse me, Miss. I have a connecting flight to Kunming. Could you tell me how to go through transfer formalities after I arrive in Beijing?

FA: (1) _____.

P: Yes, I have.

FA: (2) _____.

P: CA1156. The departure time is 2:35 p. m.

FA: (3) _____.

P: Could you tell me where the transfer counter is?

FA: (4) _____.

P: It's very kind of you.

FA: (5) _____

5. Fill in the blanks in the following sentences with the words given below. Change the form where necessary.

> destination   obtain   reconfirm   transfer   formality
> disembark   claim   domestic   reservation   spare

1) You should get your luggage back at the baggage _____ area.

2) After landing, please take your belongings with you when you _____.

3) She is already assured of the job and her interview is a mere _____.

4) Jack always manages to _____ what he wants.

5) They had a big house and a _____ bedroom where Jim could sleep.

6) It took them all day to reach their _____.

7) We'll _____ a ticket for you till next morning.

8) Do you offer an inter-bank _____ service?

9) The meeting concerns both foreign and _____ policies.

10) We must _____ whether it is true or not.

6. Complete the paragraph with the correct word in the box.

> fuel   stop   valuables   disembark   claim
> connection   departure   leave   obtain   temperature

Ladies and Gentlemen,

Our plane will be landing immediately. The local time is 2:10 p. m. , and the ground 1) _____ is about 18 degrees centigrade. We'll stop over there for about thirty minutes for 2) _____ .

　　Please make sure that your seat belt securely fastened before the plane comes to a complete 3) _____ . Passengers who are to leave the flight are requested to 4) _____ first. Please get your passport and all your belongings ready when you disembark. Your checked baggage may be claimed in the baggage 5) _____ area. If you are connecting on to other flights at this airport, please go to the 6) _____ flight counter in the waiting hall to complete the transfer formalities. Passengers who will continue to take this flight are requested to disembark and wait for 7) _____ at the boarding gate until the flight is called. Please 8) _____ your boarding card from the ground staff. You may 9) _____ your luggage on board, but take your passport and 10) _____ with you.

　　Thank you for your cooperation.

Section C   Supplementary Reading

New Passenger Transfer Facility Opened at Abu Dhabi Airport Terminal 3

Abu Dhabi International Airport today announced the opening of a transfer passenger screening facility at Terminal 3 as part of its continued Capacity Enhancement Program.

The program, which was launched in 2010, is gradually increasing the passenger handling capability at Abu Dhabi International Airport reaching an increase in the potential of the airport from the current 16 million to over 18 million passengers per annum. The new facility includes 16 new X-ray machines that will enhance transfer passengers' processing and movement from the arrival areas to the duty free and other departure facilities at the airport.

Ahmad Al Haddabi, Chief Operations Officer at Abu Dhabi Airports, said: "The Capacity Enhancement Program at our existing Terminals 1 and 3 is progressing well and cements our commitment to offering our passengers a world class travelling experience while construction of the new Midfield Terminal Complex continues at a rapid rate. Last year we witnessed record growth figures for the airport, with more than 16. 5 million passengers using our facilities, demonstrating the need for this Program to be delivered as quickly as possible in the interim. "

"The state-of-the-art X-ray machines will have a obvious effect on our transfer passengers, allowing them to spend more time enjoying our expanded and upgraded duty free outlets. The recent Skytrax Award we won for Abu Dhabi International Airport, as voted by our passengers, further motivates us to put customer service and passenger experience at the top of our list. "

Abu Dhabi International Airport is now able to channel transfer traffic into two separate screening facilities, which will drastically reduce congestion at these facilities during peak traffic times.

Questions for discussion.

1. What does the new facility include?

2. What does Ahmad Al Haddabi say about the program?

3. How many passengers used this transfer facility last year?

4. What obvious effect do X-ray machines have on transfer passengers?

5. How is the transfer traffic congestion reduced?

Section D　Interview English

Daily hot topic:

Work experience and remuneration

The typical questions on daily hot topic have been usually asked when you attend an interview. There are several examples. The answers are given for your reference.

1. Have you ever done a part-time job? What kind of job did you do?

A: Yes. I have been worked as a waitress/waiter in Kentucky/McDonald.

2. What's your opinion for a college student to do a part time job?

A: I think a college student should not do a part-time job. The most essential task of college students is study. There is no denying that doing part-time jobs assume students' study time. On the other hand, students have no experience of working at the beginning of them doing the part-time jobs so being criticized is unable to avoid. Therefore, students will lose confidence if they have received any criticism during the part-time jobs.

3. Do you think whether a college student should do a part-time job?

A: I think a college student should do a part-time job. Students can apply what they have learnt from the books to the practice, which also can strengthen their knowledge in an effective way. Besides, it is important for students to experience working and contact with society in advance, which can be prepared for their future career after they graduate.

4. If you are hired, what salary do you expect?

A: Frankly speaking, I don't know. But I am sure if I work well, you will be fair to me.

5. What's your expected salary?

A: As for salary, I leave it to you. Since this will be my first job and I don't have many experiences, I hesitate to suggest a salary. Moreover, what I value most is job satisfaction.

Role-play practice:

You want to be a flight attendant and have an interview. The interviewer asks you what salary you would expect to get. Please make an interview role-play with your partner.

Unit 11

Customs, Immigration and Quarantine

Lead-in questions

1. What will you say to a passenger if she wants to bring some fresh fruits into China?

2. What will you say to a young boy if he does not know the language in the forms?

3. How do you explain to a passenger when he wonders why he needs to fill out all kinds of forms?

Section A   Dialogues

Dialogue one

Setting: It's one hour before the landing of the flight CA1132. The flight attendant is distributing entry forms to passengers.

(*P: Passenger*)

FA: Excuse me, Sir. These are CIQ forms. Would you please fill out them before we get to New York?

P: Oh, what does CIQ stand for?

FA: It refers to Customs Immigration and Quarantine.

P: Why do we have to fill out the forms on board?

FA: You'd better do so before landing in order to save your time after arriving at the airport.

P: Do I have to return them to you after filling out them?

FA: No, now you keep them, then you will need them when you go through Immigration and Customs.

P: Well, may I fill it out in Chinese?

FA: Sorry, you have to use English. If you find it difficult in filling out these forms, I'll be pleased to help you.

P:Ok,I'm afraid you need explain some of the items for me.

FA:Go ahead,please.

P:I've bought a pair of earrings for my wife and two bottles of Maotai for my father. Do I have to pay duty for them.

FA:I think the Customs officials will let them pass.

P:Do you have any items exceeding the tax-free limit? How many cigarettes can I take into the United States? I've got 100 cigarettes with me. Is it Ok?

FA:No problem. 200 cigarettes free of duty for each otherwise you have to pay duty for the rest. If you are not sure about anything else,please refer to the back of the Customs Declaration Form for the items required for declaration.

P:Ok,should I list all taxable items,including my personal property?

FA:I suggest you'd better do it. All dutiable items which are not found on the Declaration Form will subject the owner to heavy fines.

P:Er,I see. Thank you for your service.

FA:If you still have any uncertainty,don't hesitate to tell me.

P:Oh,I take a computer with me. Should I declare it?

FA:Is it a new one?

P:No,I have used it for a long time.

FA:If it's an old one,you don't need to declare it.

P:Ok,I really appreciate what you have done for me.

FA:I'm glad I could do it.

Dialogue two

Setting:An old man seems puzzled in the cabin. He pushes the call button. A flight attendant comes up to him.

FA:Excuse me,Sir. Can I help you?

P:Yeah,I don't know how to do with these forms. It is the first time for me to enter England.

FA:Don't be worried. I'd like to help you.

P:I know a little English. What's more,I can't see them clearly as I forget to take my glasses. Would you like to explain the forms for me?

FA:I'd be pleased to. First you need to fill out your name,flight number,passport number,occupation,nationality,address and so on.

P:Even though you translate them for me, it's still difficult for me to finish them. Could you fill them out for me?

FA:OK. Yet you need tell me your information.

P:Sure. You're very nice.

FA:It's my duty. Now, let's sign this form. For the Quarantine Form, do you have a Health Certificate?

P:Yes, I do. Here you are.

FA:OK, now you keep it by yourself. In a while you just show it to the officer at the airport. Do you bring some food, including fruits, vegetables, dairy products, meat, etc?

P:Yes, I bring some fresh fruits and vegetables that my daughter likes to eat. You know my daughter likes eating Chinese cabbage very much.

FA:To comply with England Quarantine Regulations, fresh fruits, vegetables, products of animals, etc. are not allowed to be brought into the country.

P:It's a pity. My daughter can't eat delicious Chinese cabbage.

FA:What else do you bring? All the information you fill out the forms should be based on facts. British Customs officials will check the baggage of each entry passenger. If you are caught for hiding some of them, your effects will be taken away by the staff of the customs and you will leave a bad record in British Customs. By the way, do you have some stuff to declare?

P:No, I bring nothing besides my daily necessities. My visit is to see my daughter. She is working in England.

FA:I see. Sir, please sign your name here.

P:Ok, You are so patient! I don't know how to express my thanks.

FA:I enjoy assisting you. Hope you have a good trip.

Words and Expressions

distribute /dis'tribju:t/	v.	分发；分送
entry /'entri/	n.	进入，登记
refer /ri'fə:/	v.	参考；查阅
official /ə'fɪʃ(ə)l/	n.	官员
exceed /ik'si:d/	v.	超过
tax-free	a.	免税的，不付税的
Customs Declaration Form		海关申报表格
dutiable /'dju:ti:əbl/	a.	应缴税的
subject /'sʌbdʒikt/	v.	使遭受，使蒙受
uncertainty /ʌn'sɜ:tnti:/	n.	无把握；不确定
declare /di'klɛə/	v.	申报（应纳税品）
occupation /ˌɔkju'peiʃən/	n.	职业
nationality /ˌnæʃə'næliti/	n.	国籍
Health Certificate		健康证
dairy /'dɛəri/	a.	奶制的，乳品的
effects /'ifekts/	n.	财物

necessity /ni'sesiti/   *n.*   必需品

Exercises

1. Questions for discussion.

1) An old man asked " Why can't I take some fresh vegetables into China?" How can you explain it?

2) What does CIQ stand for?

3) What will you do if a passenger doesn't know the language in the forms?

4) How do you explain to a passenger why she has to fill out CIQ forms?

5) What suggestions will you give to a passenger if she doesn't know what to declare?

2. Oral Practice.

Work with a partner to make up dialogues. Situational settings are as follows.

1) When you hand out CIQ forms, a passenger does not know what to be written down in the forms. She asks for your help because she doesn't know English. You assist her to finish them.

2) This is a flight from Beijing to Boston. An old woman is going to visit her son who is studying there. She brings some food for her son. You tell her that those are not allowed to enter America according to American Quarantine Regulations.

Section B　Announcements

Announcement for Entry Forms

Ladies and Gentlemen,

We are pleased to provide you with entry forms for local Customs Immigration and Quarantine. You'd better complete them in order to save your time through Customs and Immigration. If you have any questions while finishing the forms, please don't hesitate to ask one of our flight attendants for help. They will be very pleased to assist you. When you go through the entry formalities, please submit the completed entry forms to officials from the Customs Immigration and Quarantine.

Thank you.

Announcement for Quarantine Regulations

Ladies and Gentlemen,

May I have your attention, please? According to the quarantine regulations of _____ government, passengers are not allowed to bring fresh fruits, vegetables, meat products, soil, pests, dairy products, any other plant or animal product into the country. Passengers who are in possession of such items are kindly requested to dispose of them properly and do not bring them to the aircraft.

Thank you.

Announcement for Declaration

Ladies and Gentlemen,

May I have your attention, please? All passengers must declare all plant materials or animal products within your possession. You may see notices at the airport, which will tell you what you need to declare or refer to the back of the customs declaration form for the items required for declaration. If you aren't sure about your declaration, our flight attendants will be very happy to assist you.

Thank you for your cooperation.

Words and Expressions

submit /səbˈmɪt/	v.	提交
pest /pest/	n.	害虫
possession /pəˈzeʃən/	n.	个人财产,私人财物
be in possession of		拥有、占有
dispose /dɪˈspəʊz/	v.	处理;处置;安排
dispose of		处理、解决

Exercises

1. Match the English phrases in column A with the Chinese translations in column B.

A	B
(　　) a. Health Certificate	1) 海关申报表格
(　　) b. Miat Mongolian Airlines (OM)	2) 芬兰航空公司
(　　) c. Departure Form	3) 免疫检查
(　　) d. Finnair (AY)	4) 奥林匹克航空(希腊)
(　　) e. US Airways (US)	5) 入境登记表
(　　) f. Customs Declaration Form	6) 美国合众国航空公司
(　　) g. quarantine check	7) 蒙古航空公司
(　　) h. Olympic Airways (OA)	8) 健康证
(　　) i. entry form	9) 埃塞俄比亚航空公司
(　　) j. Ethiopian Airlines (ET)	10) 出境登记表

2. Translate the following sentences into English.

1) 我想您得付 200 美元的关税。

2) 请把这份海关申报表填好并在这里签字。

3) 您到美国来的目的是什么?

4) 请将这张健康证交给出口处的官员。

5）你要在加拿大停留多久？

6）您随身携带了多少现金？

7）我能看看您的机票和护照吗？

8）请问您填这些表格有困难吗？

9）请问飞机着陆前我必须填写完 CIQ 表格吗？

10）为了节省您在机场办理入境手续的时间，您最好在飞机上完成这些表格。

3. Translate the following sentences into Chinese.

1) I've got an iphone 7 with me. Do I need to declare it?

2) I don't know English. Would you like to complete it for me?

3) Excuse me, Sir. Would you like to tell me what items I have to declare?

4) I can't find my baggage on the carousel.

5) Excuse me. I haven't got the Arrival Record Form. Could you give me one?

6) Please get your passport and carry-on bag ready for inspection.

7) Please keep your passport well, and give the declaration card to the officer at the exit.

8) I think you've made a mistake here. The type of item isn't the same as that on the declaration form.

9) Could you tell me how many cigarettes I can take into America?

10) Please read carefully the list of articles that need to be declared on the back of the form if you are not sure about anything else.

4. Suppose you are a flight attendant. Now you are distributing CIQ to every passenger before the flight gets to its destination. Passengers ask you some questions.

P：Why do we have to fill out the forms?

FA：(1)＿＿＿＿＿＿＿＿＿＿＿＿＿＿＿＿＿＿＿＿＿＿＿＿＿＿＿＿．

P：Could you tell me how to fill out the Arrival Record Form?

FA：(2)＿＿＿＿＿＿＿＿＿＿＿＿＿＿＿＿＿＿＿＿＿＿＿＿＿＿＿＿．

P：Could you help me to write them? Because I don't know English.

FA：(3)＿＿＿＿＿＿＿＿＿＿＿＿＿＿＿＿＿＿＿＿＿＿＿＿＿＿＿＿．

P：Sure. My daughter wrote my personal information on this paper. You may refer to it. If you need to learn more information, you can ask me.

FA：(4)＿＿＿＿＿＿＿＿＿＿＿＿＿＿＿＿＿＿＿＿＿＿＿＿＿＿＿＿．

P：You've been really helpful, thanks a lot.

FA：(5)＿＿＿＿＿＿＿＿＿＿＿＿＿＿＿＿＿＿＿＿＿＿＿＿＿＿＿＿．

5. Fill in the blanks in the following sentences with the words given below. Change the form where necessary.

| express declare possession distribute custom |
| submit dairy necessity exceed refer |

1) He has already _____ his resignation to his boss.

2) When you drive, you must not _____ the legal limit.

3) You can _____ to a dictionary if necessary.

4) Must I fill out the _____ declaration form?

5) Telephone is now a household _____ .

6) How are you going to _____ mail to every student?

7) Do you know how to _____ it in English?

8) That old book is father's most precious _____ .

9) Do you get anything to _____ to the customs?

10) _____ products are the best source of calcium.

6. Complete the paragraph with the correct word in the box.

> complete   passengers   understanding   provide   hesitate
> address   need   forms   declaration   note

Ladies and Gentlemen，

According to US Customs and Immigration, all arriving 1) _____ must complete (Entry and) Customs Declaration Forms.

When filling out these 2) _____, please 3) _____ that all forms must be filled out in English capital letters. You must also 4) _____ your detailed 5) _____ in American and sign the forms in person.

One family member can 6) _____ one Customs 7) _____ Form for the whole family.

If you 8) _____ any assistance, please don't 9) _____ to contact any of our flight attendants.

Thank you for your 10) _____ and cooperation.

Section C   Supplementary Reading

Canada Customs and Immigration

Entry rules to Canada are changing

Starting March 15, 2016, visa-exempt foreign nationals who fly to or transit through Canada will need an Electronic Travel Authorization (ETA). Exceptions include U. S. citizens and travellers with a valid visa.

Primary inspection

The Canada Border Services Agency (CBSA) is responsible for providing integrated border services in Canada, including customs, immigration and luggage inspection services. In major airports, CBSA agents are assisted by dog handlers and dogs that have been specially trained to detect restricted or prohibited items, such as fruit, meat and cheese, by sniffing travellers' luggage.

When you arrive in the Canada Customs hall, have your travel documents in hand as well as your completed Customs Declaration Card (E311), which you were given on the plane. The primary inspection line includes traditional customs points as well as self-service kiosks for pre-approved, low-risk travellers enrolled in the NEXUS or CANPASS Air program.

IMPORTANT!

For faster passage through Customs, Canadian citizens and Canadian permanent residents can use the new Automated Border Clearance kiosks.

You will be asked to answer a few questions, particularly with respect to the duration of your stay outside the country and the goods you are bringing back into Canada:

1. The personal exemptions to which you are entitled vary based on the duration of your stay.

2. Generally speaking, the merchandise that you may include in your personal exemption must be intended for your personal or domestic use.

3. Certain conditions apply to tobacco products and alcoholic beverages.

4. There are restrictions on firearms, food products, animals and vegetables, endangered species and cultural goods.

Baggage claim

Once customs formalities are complete, proceed to the baggage claim area and consult the illuminated display panels to find the carousel number assigned to your flight. All fragile luggage, oversized bags and pets are delivered on a specially designed conveyor belt, located on the periphery of the carousel area.

Luggage delivery is the responsibility of your air carrier. If one of your suitcases is missing or damaged, or for any other similar problem, please go to your airline's baggage service counter, located just before the baggage claim area exit.

Before leaving the terminal, double-check that the suitcases you have picked up are indeed yours. Luggage trolleys are available, free of charge, on the arrivals and departures levels at Montréal-Trudeau. You may also request assistance from a porter by contacting your airline—a representative will call a porter for you.

Secondary inspection

Before exiting into the public hall, you must give your Customs Declaration Card to a CBSA officer, who will tell you whether you need to proceed to the secondary inspection area. This consists of a manual inspection of your luggage and, in some cases, a search.

If you are travelling with a pet, you must present the animal's health report and pay the entry fees. You will also be expected to pay any fees owed in relation to your declared purchases to the cashier.

Delayed or withheld luggage

The luggage pickup service counter (for delayed or withheld items) is located in the public international arrivals hall, at the end of the corridor. Use one of the telephones provided to speak with an attendant.

Questions for discuss.

1. How are the entry rules to Canada changing?

2. What should you have in hand when you arrive in the Canada Customs hall?

3. What does the primary inspection line include?

4. What are restricted through customs?

5. Who will tell you whether you need to proceed to the secondary inspection area?

Section D   Interview English

Daily hot topic：

Success and failure

The typical questions on daily hot topic have been usually asked when you attend an interview. There are several examples. The answers are given for your reference.

1. How do you handle criticism?

A：I will accept other's criticism modestly. Because criticism not only corrects my wrong doings, but also helps me avoid mistakes.

2. Have you met failure? How to overcome it?

A：Of course. I believe in an old Chinese saying, "Failure is the mother of success." It means there is hardly any success without failure. People have to deal with many mistakes and failures in order to reach the successful finals. So failure is not a bad thing, I learn a lot from my failures.

3. How do you understand "success" and "failure"?

A：I think success brings confidence and victory. But, life is not always easy and comfortable. There are more difficulties than eases in the real life. It is likely that we have to face some failures ahead. We can get some helpful experience from failures. Therefore, those who learn how to deal with and endure failures will taste their success finally.

4. Are you afraid of facing failure?

A: No, I'm not afraid of failure. I think no one can keep from failure. If we can turn failure to our advantages, we will succeed sooner or later. Failure can be a good teacher. It can reveal that where we need improvement. So when we meet failure, we should dare to face it.

5. What are your greatest accomplishments until now?

A: I feel my greatest accomplishments are still ahead of me. Yet, I am proud of my involvement with all kinds of activities during college life. I made great contribution as part of the team and learned a lot from the activities.

Role-play practice:

You want to be a flight attendant and have an interview. The interviewer asks you what your greatest failure has been. What did you do? Please make an interview role-play with your partner.

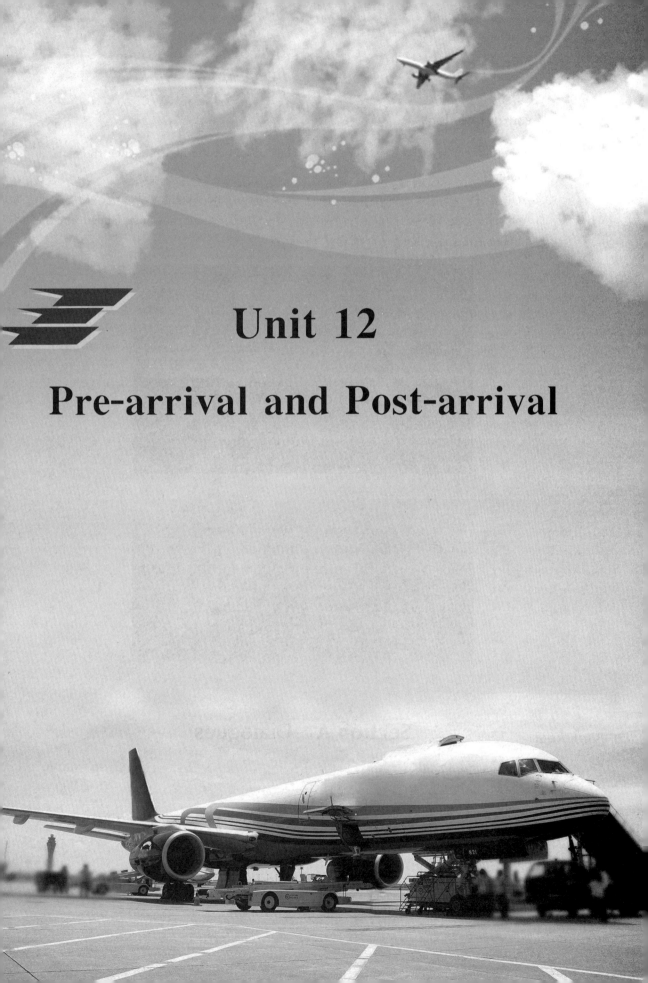

Unit 12
Pre-arrival and Post-arrival

Lead-in questions

1. What do you say to a passenger who stands up to get his luggage when the plane is taxiing?
2. What do you say to a passenger when she asks for the Baggage Claim Area?
3. What do you say to stop a passenger when the aircraft has just landed and he unfastens his seat belt?

Section A   Dialogues

Dialogue one

Setting:When the plane is taxiing on the runway,an old woman stands up to collect her baggage.

(P:Passenger)

FA:Excuse me, Madam. Please keep seated in your seat and fasten your seat belt before the plane comes to a complete stop.

P:Oh,my action is a little slow,I'm afraid that I won't have enough time to collect my belongings.

FA:Don't worry about it. I'll assist you with your belongings.

P:Ok,by the way,what's the weather like outside?

FA:It's cloudy and the temperature is 22 degrees centigrade according to the latest weather report.

P:Would you like to tell me how I can get to the city center from the airport?

FA:You can take a taxi. But I'd suggest taking the limousine. It's much cheaper and almost as fast as a taxi. It will take you into the city center.

P:How often is there a limousine?

FA:It runs every half an hour. It's very convenient.

P:How much is the fare?

FA:Twenty RMB for each one.

P:How long does it take?

FA:It will take more than one hour to get to the terminus.

P:I have made a reservation at Hilton Hotel in _____ Street. Does the limousine stop there?

FA:No,It doesn't go through there,but you may get off at the final destination which is near from your hotel,then you may go there by taxi.

P:That's a good idea. But approximately what's the taxi fare?

FA:About 10 yuan.

P:But how can I tell the taxi driver to go to my hotel? I can't speak Chinese.

FA:Oh,some taxi drivers can speak a little English. I'll write down the name of your hotel in Chinese on a piece of paper and then you just show it to the taxi driver. He'll take you there.

P:Do I have to give the taxi driver an additional tip?

FA:It's unnecessary. No tip here.

P:Thank you very much. How patient you are!

FA:Not at all.

Dialogue two

Setting:The aircraft has come to a complete stop. Most of the passengers have left the plane. At this time the flight attendant named Susan notices a man looking for something near his seat. Susan comes up to him.

Susan:Excuse me,Sir. What's wrong with you?

P:I can't find my handbag. There is a laptop in it.

Susan:I'm sorry to hear that. But don't worry. Perhaps,it's in the overhead bin or under your seat.

P: I've looked for it everywhere but found nothing.

Susan: Let me help you. Wow, Sir it's here. There is a handbag and a laptop in it. Look, please.

P: Let me see. But it's not mine. My laptop is smaller than it.

Susan: I think maybe the owner of the handbag has taken your handbag by mistake. We'll contact him immediately.

P: You must help me find my handbag because there is some important information in my laptop. It's really very important for me.

Susan: We'll do our utmost to help you. What else is there in your handbag?

P: No, only a laptop.

Susan: Please remain calm. Would you mind leaving your name, address and telephone number?

P: OK, I'm Simon. The hotel address is No. 388, _____ street, _____ district, Beijing. The telephone number is 139 _____ . My handbag is black and the laptop is silver.

Susan: All right. We'll get contact with you if we have any information about it.

P: I'm very much obliged to you for your help. By the way, where is the baggage claim area? I'll have to get my checked baggage.

Susan: When you disembark, the baggage claim area is in the arrival hall. When you arrive, you will see the signs pointing to the baggage claim area. You may follow them then you will find there.

P: Would you mind telling me where Shangri-la hotel is? How can I get there quickly? I will attend an international meeting there, but I'm afraid I will be late.

Susan: You can hire a cab right outside the terminal. Hiring a cab is faster than taking an airport bus, but it's more expensive. When does your meeting begin?

P: 2:00 p. m.

Susan: Oh, only one hour left. You'd better take a cab to go there.

P: Ok, I'm extremely grateful to you.

Susan: Don't mention it. It's our duty to do this.

Words and Expressions

limousine /ˈlimuziːn/	n.	（往返机场接送旅客的）中型客车
terminus /ˈtɜːminəs/	n.	终点站
approximately /əˈprɒksimitli/	ad.	大约
additional /əˈdiʃnl/	a.	额外的
oblige /əˈblaidʒ/	v.	使感激

hire /ˈhaiə/	v.	雇用
cab /kæb/	n.	出租车
grateful /ˈgreitful/	a.	感激的，感谢的

Exercises

1. Questions for discussion.

1) When the aircraft hasn't come to a complete stop, a passenger unfastens her seat belt. What do you say to stop her?

2) What will you say if a passenger asks how he can get into the city from the airport?

3) How do you tell a passenger where the baggage claim hall is?

4) What should a flight attendant do before the plane is landing?

5) What should a flight attendant do after the plane lands?

2. Oral Practice.

Work with a partner to make up dialogues. Situational settings are as follows.

1) The plane will be landing at the destination airport in about 30 minutes. You tell passengers to make preparation for landing. A passenger is still using his computer and unfastens his seat belt. You remind all passengers of fastening their seat belts and turning off all electronic devices.

2) Now the plane is taxiing on the runway. The passengers are excited. Some stand up from their seats and some try to get their baggage from the overhead bins. You ask the passengers to return to their seats and fasten their seat belts until the plane comes to a complete stop.

Section B　Announcements

Pre-arrival Announcement

Ladies and Gentlemen,

May I have your attention please? Our plane will be landing at Beijing International Airport in about 15 minutes. As we are ready for landing, all passengers, please return to your seats, fasten your seat belts and put your seats back and put your tables to the upright position. Please don't use the toilets. For passengers sitting by the windows, will you please open the window shades? All electronic devices must be turned off at this time. You mustn't turn on your mobile phones and unfasten your seat belts until the plane comes to a complete stop.

On behalf of the captain and all our crew, we would like to thank you for your support and cooperation during the flight. We hope you enjoy your flight with us.

Post-arrival Announcement

Ladies and Gentlemen,

Our plane has landed at London Heathrow International Airport. It is sunny outside now and temperature is _____ degree centigrade or _____ degrees Fahrenheit. The distance between the airport and downtown is 30km. Please don't unfasten your seat belts before the "fasten seat belt" sign goes off and do not open your overhead compartments. Please make sure to collect all your belongings when you disembark. Your checked baggage may be claimed in the terminal building.

If you are connecting or transferring to another flight, please contact the check-in counter and complete your transit formalities in the airport transit counter.

On behalf of the entire crew, I would like to thank you for flying with British Airway. We look forward to having the opportunity to serve you in the future.

Words and Expressions

window shades		遮光板
support /sə'pɔːt/	*n.*	支持
check-in counter		办理登机手续的柜台
entire /in'taɪə/	*a.*	全体的

Exercises

1. Match the English phrases in column A with the Chinese translations in column B.

A	B
( ) a. window shade	1) 摆渡车
( ) b. Qantas Airways (QF)	2) 缅甸国际航空公司
( ) c. ground staff	3) 办理登机手续的柜台
( ) d. Scandinavian Airlines (SK)	4) 澳洲航空公司
( ) e. luggage carousel	5) 行李传送带
( ) f. check-in counter	6) 荷兰皇家航空公司
( ) g. KLM Royal Dutch Airlines (KL)	7) 遮光板
( ) h. ferry bus	8) 波兰航空公司
( ) i. Lot-Polish Airlines (LO)	9) 地面工作人员
( ) j. Myanmar Airways (UB)	10) 斯堪的纳维亚航空公司

2. Translate the following sentences into English.

1) 我们的飞机正准备降落。为了您的安全,请系好安全带。

2) 我们抱歉地通知您,由于北京地区有大雾,我们不得不改落天津机场。

3) 您的托运行李须到行李认领处认领。

4) 感谢您乘坐我们的航班,希望有幸能与您再次见面。

5）如果您还有转接班机的话，必须在报关后去国内候机楼等候。

6）感谢您在旅途中对我们工作的支持和配合。

7）本次航班预计在 20 分钟后到达香港国际机场。

8）目的地机场天空晴朗，地面温度是 25 摄氏度。

9）先生您好，您的箱子上有什么明显的标志吗？我们会尽最大努力帮您查找的。

10）大件的行李和不规则行李都是在那边的柜台提取。

3. Translate the following sentences into Chinese.

1）I will make a stopover in Shanghai. Would you recommend me to do anything?

2）What's the time of departure? Is there any change?

3）I have made a reservation at Home-in Hotel. Would you tell me where it is?

4）Is it very convenient to take a ferry bus after I arrive?

5）Could you tell me the weather condition at the destination airport?

6）We are very sorry for that. When your suitcase arrives, we will contact you as soon as possible and deliver it to you.

7）All of the baggage have been sent out. Everyone took them out.

8）Excuse me, Mrs. I can't find my luggage, could you please help me to check it?

9）As I know, no bus goes there directly. You may take a taxi outside the terminal building.

10）The airplane has already stopped. Now please get your belongings ready to disembark.

4. Suppose you are a flight attendant. The plane has come to a complete stop. You are busy helping passengers with their baggage.

FA：Ladies and gentlemen, the plane has already stopped. Please disembark with your belongings.

P：Where is the exit?

FA：(1) _____.

P：How can I get to the arrival hall?

FA：(2) _____.

P：Do I need to pay money?

FA：(3) _____.

P：Where can I get my checked baggage?

FA：(4) _____.

P：That's fine. Thank you.

FA：(5) _____.

5. Fill in the blanks in the following sentences with the words given below. Change the form where necessary.

> terminus additional opportunity limousine utmost
> oblige hire grateful support approximately

1) I'm so _____ to you for spending the whole day chatting with us.

2) Thanks for your _____ and guidance in this job.

3) Her income _____ five thousand dollars a year.

4) The storm got worse and worse. Finally, I was _____ to abandon the car and continue on foot.

5) The president _____ two painters to paint all classrooms.

6) We will try our _____ to get this chance.

7) He fell asleep in the bus and was taken on to the _____.

8) I take this _____ of thanking you for your help.

9) They rented a _____ to travel in the city.

10) The system can provide _____ information as well.

6. Complete the paragraph with the correct word in the box.

> fastened sunny understanding tray devices
> disembark prepare behalf remind return

Ladies and Gentlemen,

We will be landing at Beijing International Airport in about 15 minutes. It is 1) _____ outside now and temperature is 30 degree celsius. As we 2) _____ for landing please 3) _____ your seat back to the upright position, take back your 4) _____ table, and keep your seat belt 5) _____ until the plane comes to a complete stop. All electronic 6) _____ must be turned off when the plane is landing. We would also 7) _____ you to take all your belongings when you 8) _____.

On 9) _____ of all our crew members, I'd like to thank you for your 10) _____ and cooperation during the whole flight. Have a good trip!

Section C   Supplementary Reading

How to Claim Compensation for Lost, Delayed or Damaged Luggage

If your luggage is delayed, goes missing or gets damaged on a flight, what sort of compensation are you entitled to? The Montreal Convention makes airlines responsible for the bags they allow you to check in, although their liability is limited to around £ 1 113 per passenger.

Act immediately

Airlines are more likely to accept responsibility for missing or damaged luggage if you report the problem straightaway. Before leaving the luggage reclaim hall, go to the airline desk.

Fill out a form

You'll be given a copy of the Property Irregularity Report (PIR) that's used by airline staff to record the details. While this isn't a legal requirement, and there maybe a reason why it's not possible to get one (an unmanned desk at a small airport, for example) you're still entitled to claim. But without a PIR, the process is likely to be more of an uphill battle.

If the bag is damaged

If you want to claim compensation, write to the airline within seven days of receiving your luggage, enclosing a copy of the PIR. You will need a PIR form before you claim for any luggage irregularities.

If the bag is missing

As well as personal and flight details, you'll need to give an accurate description of a missing bag, recording any distinguishing features. A good tip (for the highly organized) is to keep a photo of your luggage on your phone in case you ever need to make this sort of report. Photographic evidence can also help if you are reporting damaged luggage.

Observe the deadlines

Write to the airline, enclosing the copy of the PIR, within seven days of the flight. If your luggage turns up a day or two late, it's up to the airline to make arrangements for getting it to you as efficiently as possible.

Monitor progress

Where luggage doesn't show up, you should be able to monitor it through the tracing procedure, either by contacting baggage services at the airport or by logging into an online baggage-tracing page with a reference number. This reference will relate to the luggage receipt usually attached to your passport or boarding card at check-in or bag-drop, so you'll need to keep it to hand. If there's no sign of it after three weeks, the bag will be declared lost. At the end of a long flight, the last thing you want to see is an empty baggage carousel.

Check the rules

If your bag has gone missing on the outward flight and you find you're on holiday with no possessions, airlines are obliged to cover costs of "essential items". However, this definition can be a sticking point when it comes to compensation. Depending on the attitude of the airline, it may argue that "essential items" are classified as toiletries, underwear or laundry costs rather than a brand new outfit. In most cases the airline will track down your bag quickly and return it to you within a couple of days.

Make a claim

Ask the airline what its policy is and keep receipts for anything you buy. A potential compensation is when your bag has been transferred to another one or two airlines within a single journey. In this case it makes sense to claim from the last one flown, as it's this airline which usually handles the claim.

A claim for a delayed bag must be sent to the airline's customer relations department within 21 days of handing your luggage to the airline. Depending on various factors such as how complicated your claim is, and the time of year, it may take as long as a couple of months to process.

To claim compensation for missing bag, you must write to the airline within seven days of the luggage being declared lost.

Check your insurance policy

However, you're likely to find the airline tries to pass the buck by suggesting you take the issue of compensation up with your travel insurer. Depending on your policy, you may get a higher level of cover this way. Be sure to check your insurer's excess charge and small print first—some policies provide minimal or no cover for luggage while in the care of an airline.

Questions for discussion.

1. According to the passage, how to act immediately if the luggage is missing or damaged?
2. What is PIR used for?
3. What is the good tip if the luggage is missing?
4. What should you do if the luggage didn't show up?
5. When must you write to claim for the compensation for the missing bag?

Section D   Interview English

Daily hot topic:

Ending an interview

The typical questions on daily hot topic have been usually asked when you attend an interview. There are several examples. The answers are given for your reference.

1. Are there any questions you would like to ask about the position or the company?

A: Yes, would you tell me how many people you are planning to hire?

2. Is there any other information I need provide?

A: No. Thank you for your time, and I'll wait for your good news.

3. Shall we notify you of our decision by mail or phone?

A: Either will do. My address and telephone number are written on my resume.

4. We will inform you by phone within a week if you are accepted. Good-bye.

A: Thank you for this interview. I'll wait to hear from you.

5. That's all for the interview. Please wait for our notification.

A: I'm very grateful for your interview with me.

Role-play practice:

You want to be a flight attendant and have an interview. Do you think what kind of questions the interviewer will ask you? Please make an interview role-play with your partner.

References

[1] 高锋 . 航空乘务英语教程[M]. 上海:同济大学出版社,2013.

[2] 黎富玉 . 民航空乘英语[M]. 北京:北京大学出版社 . 2008.

[3] 李桂兰,陈磊 . 民航服务英语[M]. 上海:复旦大学出版社,2015.

[4] 李文静 . 机场、空乘服务实用英语对话及词汇手册[M]. 北京:中国水利水电出版社,2010.

[5] 李勇 . 新编民航乘务员实用英语[M]. 北京:中国民航出版社,2009.

[6] 林扬 . 民航乘务英语会话[M]. 北京:旅游教育出版社,2014.

[7] 王远梅 . 空乘英语[M]. 北京:国防工业出版社,2011.

[8] 俞涛 . 民航服务英语[M]. 北京:中国民航出版社,2011.

[9]《民航乘务英语》教材编写组 . 民航乘务英语[M]. 北京:高等教育出版社,2006.

Appendix

The Key to the Exercises

Unit 1　Preparation for the Flight

1. Choose the correct translations in column B to match with column A.

a. 8)　　　　b. 9)　　　　c. 1)　　　　d. 6)　　　　e. 4)

f. 2)　　　　g. 10)　　　　h. 7)　　　　i. 5)　　　　j. 3)

2. Translate the following sentences into English.

1) Let's begin our preflight briefing. I'm the chief purser of today's flight.

2) Who can tell me how many passengers are checked in first class and economy class?

3) I'm very glad to be here to work with you today.

4) We are a team, thus we should cooperate with each other during the whole flight.

5) The flying distance is 5,600km and the flight time will last about 7 hours.

6) There is time difference between Beijing and New York. Please try to adjust to it.

7) This is your purser Mary. On behalf of Air China Airlines, I'd like to welcome you aboard our CA783 from Beijing to London.

8) The safety of aircraft and passengers on board is the main responsibility for a flight attendant.

9) A qualified flight attendant must have a lofty goal and passion.

10) Peter and I will be responsible for the first class and business class; the others will be in charge of the economy class.

3. Translate the following sentences into Chinese.

1) 请根据规定,操作分配器手柄,并确保进行互检。

2) 现在我们互相认识一下,当我叫您的名字时请举手。

3) 乘客登机时我们要用甜美的微笑给乘客留下一个美好的印象。

4) 请帮我检查一下娱乐设备是否都好用。

5) 请为睡觉的乘客留餐,不要叫醒他们。

6) 根据航空服务规定,我们大约在 12 点钟提供午餐,而不是饮料服务后提供午餐。

7) 到了关闭音乐、欢迎旅客登机的时间了。

8) 对于一名乘务员来说,即使是航前也有大量准备工作要做。

9) 登机后请检查紧急设备并汇报给乘务长。

10) 地面温度最高 34℃,最低 19℃。

4. The cabin crew greet each other at the preflight briefing. Please fill in the blanks of the following dialogue.

(PS＝purser, FA＝flight attendant)

1) Nice to meet you, too.

2) First, let me introduce myself. My name is Zhang Yifei. Glad to meet you!

3) How do you do, everybody? My name is Wu Qiong.

4) I am very happy to meet everyone. My name is Zhang Shuo.

5) I am very glad to meet everyone. My name is Wang Xiaoyu. Thank you.

5. Fill in the blanks in the following sentences with the words given below. Change the form where necessary.

1) sufficient　　2) estimate　　3) seniors　　4) check　　5) qualification

6) remained　　7) Equipment　8) assign　　9) counter　　10) cooperation

6. Complete the paragraph with the correct word in the box.

1) aware　　　2) regards　　3) provide　　4) safety　　5) responsibility

6) qualified　　7) patient　　8) important　9) communicate　10) fluently

Unit 2   Passenger Reception

1. Choose the correct translations in column B to match with column A.

a. 7)　　　　b. 5)　　　　c. 8)　　　　d. 9)　　　　e. 3)

f. 1)　　　　g. 2)　　　　h. 10)　　　　i. 4)　　　　j. 6)

2. Translate the following sentences into English.

1) What's your seat number? May I see your boarding pass, please?

2) I'm afraid the man might be in the wrong seat. Please wait a moment here.

3) Excuse me, Sir. Is there anything I can do for you? I see your call button on.

4) Excuse me, Madam. Could you hold your baby outside the seat belt? That'll be comfortable for your baby.

5) Luggage couldn't be placed here as the aisle mustn't be blocked.

6) It is my first time to travel by air so I'm very nervous.

7) Excuse me, Mrs. My name is Mary. I am in charge of the first class. If there is anything I can do for you, please don't hesitate to call me.

8) All our crew members will be happy to be of service to you.

9) Please place your carry-on luggage in the overhead compartment or under the seat in front of you.

10) Do you see the aisle seat next to the emergency exit over there?

3. Translate the following sentences into Chinese.

1) 小姐,你好。那边的女孩是我的女朋友,她有点头晕和恶心,我想知道我能否坐在她旁边。

2) 为了确保飞机起飞时的配载平衡,您应坐在指定的位置上。

3) 我的手提包不知道该放在哪儿,行李架已满,我试着放在座位下面,但放不下。你能帮我一下吗?

4）我看看，您的座位号是 20A，在客舱的中部。你看到那边出口靠窗户的座位了吗？

5）您介意帮我调一下空调吗？凉风正吹在我头上，我感到有点冷。

6）座位号码就在每个舱顶行李箱边缘。

7）老人跟着乘务员来到他的座位，但发现他的座位上有个女孩。

8）我可以调到公务舱吗？经济舱太吵了。

9）那边的那个男孩是我的朋友，我想同他坐在一起。

10）乘务员你好，我可以坐那个空座吗？这个空间太小了，我伸不开腿。

4. Suppose you are a flight attendant. Now you are showing an old man to his seat and help him arrange his baggage. Please fill in the blanks of the following dialogue.

1）May I see your boarding card? I will show you where your seat is. Your seat is 18B. Follow me, please.

2）You may put it in the overhead bin or under your seat in front of you.

3）Of course.

4）Wait a moment, please. I will bring a piece of blanket for you.

5）I'd glad I could do it. /It's my pleasure. /It's our duty to do this.

5. Fill in the blanks in the following sentences with the words given below. Change the form where necessary.

1）dizzy   2）cooperated   3）creased   4）valuables   5）deplaned

6）identified   7）purser   8）allow   9）hesitate   10）altitude

6. Complete the paragraph with the correct word in the box.

1）distance   2）take   3）altitude   4）fasten   5）electronic

6）ensure   7）compartment 8）remind   9）assistance 10）journey

Unit 3   Safety Check before Take-off

1. Choose the correct translations in column B to match with column A.

a. 7）   b. 6）   c. 10）   d. 1）   e. 8）

f. 2）   g. 5）   h. 9）   i. 4）   j. 3）

2. Translate the following sentences into English.

1）Please securely fasten your seat belt when the seat belt sign illuminates.

2）There are several emergency exits on this aircraft. Please locate the one nearest to you if you need to evacuate the aircraft.

3）Please return your seat back, footrest to the original position for take-off and landing.

4）If you are sitting in a window seat, please help us open the sunshade.

5）In order to ensure the normal operation of airplane navigation and communication system,you are kindly requested to switch off all the electronic devices.

6）Please fasten your seat belts,especially during taxing,take-off and landing.

7）Please put out your cigarette immediately. Smoking is not allowed during the whole flight.

8）We will show you the use of life vest,seatbelt,and oxygen mask.

9）The aircraft is landing so it's dangerous to leave your seat. Please keep your seat belt fastened.

10）Please refer to the safety instructions in the seat pocket in front of you for further information.

3. Translate the following sentences into Chinese.

1）请大家检查一下安全带是否系好,椅背是否放直,小桌板是否收起来。

2）请您把座椅背放直好吗？只要按一下您扶手上的按钮即可。

3）请将您的行李放在头顶上方的行李架上或您座位前的座椅下。

4）飞机起飞和着陆期间卫生间暂停使用。

5）根据规定,为了确保机舱环境的清洁和舒适,机上禁止吸烟。

6）机舱里如果需要氧气,氧气面罩会自动从您头顶上方的行李箱里脱落在你面前。

7）如果出现紧急情况,地面上的指示灯会指向紧急出口。

8）您能告诉我如何系紧安全带吗？

9）我们的飞机马上就要起飞,请确保系好安全带,调直座椅靠背。

10）您的救生衣就在您座椅底下或舱顶的行李箱里。

4. Suppose you are a flight attendant. Now you are serving an unaccompanied child in the cabin. She doesn't fasten her seat belt. Please fill in the blanks of the following dialogue.

1）Would you like to help me? /How can I fasten it?

2）Ok. / Er. it's too tight. Would you loosen it a little?

3）Please securely fasten your seat belt when the seat belt sign illuminates.

4）We'll arrive at Beijing International Airport at nine o'clock.

5）Thank you very much. / Thanks a lot.

5. Fill in the blanks in the following sentences with the words given below. Change the form where necessary.

1）interfering   2）secured   3）diverted   4）ditching   5）relieve

6）adjust   7）turbulence   8）loosened   9）inflated   10）automatically

6. Complete the paragraph with the correct word in the box.

1）introduce   2）belt   3）necessary   4）signs   5）ditches

6）inflate   7）blow   8）appear   9）emergency   10）information

Unit 4　Reasons for Delay

1. Choose the correct translations in column B to match with column A.

a. 8)　　　　b. 9)　　　　c. 6)　　　　d. 7)　　　　e. 10)

f. 5)　　　　g. 2)　　　　h. 4)　　　　i. 1)　　　　j. 3)

2. Translate the following sentences into English.

1) We are sorry to inform you that your flight will be canceled due to mechanical reasons.

2) Excuse me, how long will we wait for CA560 heading for New York to take off?

3) We can't take off for the airport is closed due to poor visibility.

4) We have to wait for taking off until the ice on the runway has been cleared.

5) The plane will take off as soon as the weather gets better.

6) The flight will be delayed about an hour because of the ground heavy fog.

7) We will notify you at once as soon as we get further information.

8) I'm afraid we have to wait until the weather gets better at the airport.

9) Several aircrafts are waiting for taking off due to the air traffic congestion on the runway.

10) Flight CA5645 has been canceled due to bad weather condition at the destination airport.

3. Translate the following sentences into Chinese.

1) 给您带来的不便,我们深表歉意。我建议您现在改签下一个航班。

2) 由于今晚 MF5688 次航班已取消,我们将在这里过夜,请拿好随身物品准备下飞机。

3) 别担心,过一会我们将为每一位乘客提供免费食宿。

4) 由于空中交通管制,我们要等通行许可才能起飞。

5) 我们刚刚得到沈阳桃仙国际机场的最新消息,9C6580 次航班延误。

6) 要是航班延误的话,你不得不在机场再等 4 个小时乘下一个航班。

7) 我们很抱歉地通知您,您的航班到达时间将要延误到晚上 6 点半。

8) 我们已经接到通知,由于技术故障,登机时间将要推迟。

9) 打扰一下先生,飞机起飞已经延误一个多小时了,航班出什么问题了?

10) 天气复杂多变,请您关注关于您的航班的最新广播。

4. Suppose you are an airport crew. Now a plane is delayed at the airport for 40 minutes. You explain the situation to the passengers. Please fill in the blanks of the following dialogue.

1) The reason is unknown at the moment. /we don't get reason. /The delay is due to some technical reasons/ bad weather condition/air traffic control/poor visibility at the airport.

2) I'm terribly sorry for the delay. I don't know either. We will inform you once the time is fixed. /The delay will be 30 minutes.

3) Sorry for the inconvenience brought to you.

4) It doesn't matter. I'd like to help you. Follow me please.

5) It's my duty.

5. Fill in the blanks in the following sentences with the words given below. Change the form where necessary.

1) schedule   2) mechanical   3) departure   4) overcame   5) clearance

6) thunderstorm 7) delay   8) congested   9) button   10) inconvenience

6. Complete the paragraph with the correct word in the box.

1) inform   2) congestion   3) runway   4) fairly   5) depart

6) clearance   7) belongings   8) staff   9) lounge   10) information

Unit 5   Drink and Meal Service

1. Choose the correct translations in column B to match with column A.

a. 3)   b. 4)   c. 1)   d. 5)   e. 2)

f. 10)   g. 8)   h. 7)   i. 6)   j. 9)

2. Translate the following sentences into English.

1) What would you like to drink, Madam? Coffee, fruit juice or hot tea?

2) On today's flight, we will provide you with cold drinks, mineral water, fruit juice, Sprite and Cola. The hot drinks like coffee, black tea and hot water are also available.

3) Excuse me, Sir, do you need any more drinks?

4) We don't accept any tips. It's our duty to serve the passengers. Thank you.

5) I'm awfully sorry. We haven't coffee on board now. Would you like to try some green tea?

6) How do you like your steak done? Rare, medium or well-done?

7) Here is today's menu. What would you like to have?

8) Which would you like for lunch, chicken, beef or fish?

9) Please open your tray table. Lunch is coming.

10) Have you finished your meal? May I clear up your tray table?

3. Translate the following sentences into Chinese.

1) 打扰一下,小姐,你们什么时候供应饮料,我有点渴了。

2) 你们都有些什么喝的?

3) 你能告诉我什么时候供应午餐吗?

4) 我要一杯咖啡都要了三次了,还要等多久?

5）很抱歉地告知您目前没有热饮。

6）小姐,打扰一下,什么时候供晚餐呀? 我都已经饿了。

7）我想要牛肉饭,而不是鸡肉面条。

8）整个飞行期间,客舱所提供的美味佳肴和优质的服务给我留下了深刻印象。

9）我很享受这顿晚餐。牛肉非常鲜嫩。

10）打扰一下,先生,因为我不吃猪肉,所以我提前订了一份穆斯林餐,我的午餐什么时候能来?

4. Suppose you are a flight attendant. Now you are serving drinks on board. Please fill in the blanks of the following dialogue.

1）We have cold and hot drinks. Which would you prefer?

2）I'd like to have coffee with a little sugar.

3）It's very kind of you.

4）Please wait a moment. After a while, we will serve you starters.

5）Of course.

5. Fill in the blanks in the following sentences with the words given below. Change the form where necessary.

1）provides   2）available   3）switch   4）awfully   5）prefers

6）prohibits   7）reminds   8）fare   9）offered   10）entirely

6. Complete the paragraph with the correct word in the box.

1）attention   2）cabin   3）choice   4）put   5）convenience

6）return   7）diet   8）press   9）effort   10）trip

Unit 6　Special Passengers Service

1. Choose the correct translations in column B to match with column A.

a. 10)   b. 7)   c. 2)   d. 6)   e. 8)

f. 3)   g. 4)   h. 1)   i. 9)   j. 5)

2. Translate the following sentences into English.

1）Don't worry. You can relieve your earache by eating gums in your mouth.

2）I hope you will feel better after taking some medicine. Please take a nap.

3）Excuse me, Madam. If you want to sleep, you'd better fasten your seat belt for your safety.

4）May I have your attention, please? There is a sick passenger on board. If there is a doctor or nurse, please contact our crew members.

5）The airsickness bag is found in your seat pocket. If you feel sick, please use it.

6）I will bring a blanket and a pillow for you. Perhaps you'll feel better after a nap.

7) I'm afraid I am a little airsick. Would you like to take some airsick tablets for me?

8) We have informed the ground staff and they'll take you to the hospital as soon as you reach the airport.

9) I really can't thank you enough for everything you've done for me.

10) Excuse me, Mrs. I still feel nauseous and uncomfortable now. Would you like to help me?

3. Translate the following sentences into Chinese.

1) 我的胃很痛。请问机舱上有止痛药吗?

2) 我好像感冒了,鼻塞并且头也痛。

3) 我想去洗手间,请问你能给我提供一个轮椅吗?

4) 我感到有点晕和恶心,你能给我来杯热水吗?

5) 别担心,我将广播为您找大夫,当您到达机场时将为您安排救护车。

6) 您能描述一下症状吗? 或许我能在飞机上帮您解决问题。

7) 如果您觉得恶心想吐,可以使用您前面座椅口袋里的晕机袋。

8) 我感到胸闷头晕并且呼吸困难。

9) 前舱有些空座,我可以把手扶抬起让您躺下休息。

10) 机上有位严重的病人,所以机长决定在杭州机场进行紧急着陆。

4. Suppose you are a flight attendant. Now a passenger is suffering from airsickness. He presses the call button. Please fill in the blanks of the following dialogue.

1) That's too bad. According to experience, you are suffering from airsickness.

2) I haven't airsick tablets. What can I do with it?

3) You can relieve your earache by swallowing and by chewing gums.

4) I will have a try. Thank you.

5) Not at the moment.

5. Fill in the blanks in the following sentences with the words given below. Change the form where necessary.

1) emergency   2) terrible   3) swallow   4) disabled   5) symptom

6) ensure   7) appreciate   8) contact   9) nauseous   10) considerate

6. Complete the paragraph with the correct word in the box.

1) route   2) provinces   3) cross   4) carry   5) button

6) located   7) rear   8) remind   9) prohibited   10) beverages

Unit 7   Emergency Procedures

1. Choose the correct translations in column B to match with column A.

a. 6)   b. 5)   c. 2)   d. 9)   e. 7)

f. 4)   g. 3)   h. 10)   i. 1)   j. 8)

2. Translate the following sentences into English.

1) This plane has eight emergency exits. Please locate the exit nearest to you.

2) Because the plane meets severe turbulence, please fasten your seat belts at once.

3) Bend down and place your head between your knees, then grab your knees.

4) Bring seat backs to the upright position and stow all tray tables, straight up your footrest.

5) Don't inflate the life jacket in the cabin. Please inflate it by pulling down the red tab as soon as you leave the aircraft.

6) The lavatories have been closed because the plane is encountering severe turbulence.

7) Don't be worried. Please keep calm. Our captain has full competence and confidence to land the plane safely.

8) There is a possibility that our plane will have to stay overnight at this alternate airport.

9) The plane will make an emergency landing due to the oil leakage.

10) You aren't allowed to release your seat belts until the plane comes to a complete stop.

3. Translate the following sentences into Chinese.

1) 先生，你好，刚才我太紧张了，没弄清楚怎么回事，你能再给我展示一下吗？

2) 你能告诉我上海浦东国际机场的天气情况吗？

3) 你能帮我抱一下我儿子吗？我穿上救生衣。

4) 小姐，打扰一下。如果我不想乘飞机，我的票能退吗？

5) 已经晚点 20 分钟了，飞机出什么事了吗？

6) 为了您的安全，请在撤离时除掉您的尖锐物品，例如耳环、手表、笔和高跟鞋等。

7) 我会让我的同事尽快给您拿个氧气瓶。

8) 由于技术故障，机舱失压。请拉下氧气面罩，放在口鼻处。

9) 我们所有的工作人员对这种情况都接受过良好的训练。请认真听从我们的指挥。

10) 机上每位乘务人员最重要的职责就是时刻确保每位乘客的安全。

4. Suppose you are a flight attendant. Now the captain has decided to make an emergency landing. You are working as a flight attendant to help the passengers in the cabin. Please fill in the blanks of the following dialogue.

1) The plane will make an emergency landing because of the bad weather conditions/ the mechanical reasons/the overheated engines.

2) Don't worry! Our captain has confidence to land safely. Please follow our instructions.

3) Of course. Let me help you to put it.

4) Don't panic. All the crew members of this flight are well trained for this kind of situation.

5) Sorry. The toilets have been closed as the plane is making an emergency landing.

5. Fill in the blanks in the following sentences with the words given below. Change the form where necessary.

1) evacuated   2) rescued   3) damage   4) unfavorable   5) agency

6) competent   7) calmly   8) leakage   9) comforted   10) scared

6. Complete the paragraph with the correct word in the box.

1) emergency   2) captain   3) inform   4) preparation   5) instructions

6) upright   7) remove   8) safety   9) inflate   10) keep

Unit 8   In-flight Entertainment

1. Choose the correct translations in column B to match with column A.

a. 7)   b. 5)   c. 10)   d. 1)   e. 8)

f. 9)   g. 2)   h. 3)   i. 6)   j. 4)

2. Translate the following sentences into English.

1) Would you like to read some newspaper or magazines?

2) We have *China Daily*, *Financial Times*, *CAAC Journal*, *New York times* and some local papers. Which one would you prefer?

3) We will show a film, pop music, folk music, classic music and Beijing opera.

4) We are sorry that the video system is not available on this flight, but you can have a wide selection of audio programs.

5) We will land at London International Airport. Our in-flight entertainment programs have now been concluded.

6) Would you like to give me several English newspapers or magazines? I want to look through them.

7) For our passengers in First and Business class, you will find your personal television in your armrest.

8) Excuse me, Sir. Can you tell me which movie is showing now?

9) Please press the button on your armrest then select the channel that you like.

10) By the way, do you have any recommendation about the movie today?

3. Translate the following sentences into Chinese.

1) 打扰一下，先生，我不知道怎么用耳麦，你能给我展示一下吗？

2) 小姐，麻烦一下，我的一个耳麦不响了，你能给我换一个吗？

3) 打扰一下，我想读点什么。你们有英文报纸或杂志吗？

4) 你能帮我调一下吗？我想看电影。

5) 小姐，你能给我推荐一下今天的电影吗？

6）航班上你可以免费从乘务员那里获得耳机。

7）请选择你想看的电影频道或想听的音乐频道。

8）我很喜欢这副耳机，可以把它带回家吗？

9）如果您想看电视或听音乐，耳机就在您前面的座椅口袋里。

10）非常抱歉，这台电视现在不能正常运行了，我在核查是否有别的座位给您调换。

4. Suppose you are a flight attendant. Now a woman with a little boy asks for your help. She asks if there are any entertainments for children on board. You are working as a flight attendant to help the passengers in the cabin. Please fill in the blanks of the following dialogue according to your understanding.

1）Yeah, we have all kinds of story-books, toys and crayons. What's more, he can listen to nursery rhymes or watch animated movies.

2）You are welcome. / It is our duty to serve you well.

3）No problem. What film does your son like watching?

4）Sure. We have a comedy movie called *Home Alone* which is very funny. I think your son will like it.

5）I adjust it at once. Please enjoy it with your son.

5. Fill in the blanks in the following sentences with the words given below. Change the form where necessary.

1）comedy   2）correspond   3）pop   4）classical   5）enrich

6）digest   7）acquired   8）recommendation   9）presented

10）assistance

6. Complete the paragraph with the correct word in the box.

1）show   2）choice   3）acquired   4）charge   5）corresponds

6）watching   7）listen   8）requirement   9）hesitate   10）enjoy

Unit 9   Duty Free Sales

1. Choose the correct translations in column B to match with column A.

a. 4）   b. 6）   c. 9）   d. 8）   e. 3）

f. 7）   g. 10）   h. 1）   i. 2）   j. 5）

2. Translate the following sentences into English.

1）In an effort to further meet our travelling needs, we will offer you a good selection of duty-free goods on board.

2）Please ask for the flight attendant's help if you want to know the prices in other currencies.

3) You have many choices, such as candy, toys, cartoon books and so on.

4) I'm sorry all the items we sell on board are sold at a marked price.

5) We regret that we don't accept checks. You have to pay in cash or by credit card.

6) Excuse me, Mrs. Do you sell duty-free goods on board?

7) Excuse me, Sir. Would you like to buy any duty-free items?

8) This cosmetic is too expensive. Can you give me a discount?

9) A duty-free brochure is in the seat pocket in front of you. You may look through it.

10) All the items sold on board are priced in US dollars.

3. Translate the following sentences into Chinese.

1) 美元和人民币之间的汇率是多少?

2) 你能给我推荐一件礼物给我儿子吗?

3) 我听说人头马 X. O. 酒很有名,我一直想尝尝。

4) 我听说中国的丝绸很有名,我正好想买,你能给我介绍吗?

5) 恐怕这个颜色不太适合我的妻子,有粉色的吗?

6) 我们不接受小费,为您服务是我们的职责。

7) 我没有足够的零钱找您,请稍等,我马上回来。

8) 请问我可以带多少瓶酒到中国?

9) 我想给我父亲买点威士忌作为礼物,先生,你们都有什么威士忌?

10) 我想知道购买免税品需要什么货币支付?

4. Suppose you are a flight attendant. A gentleman wants to know what kind of duty free goods you have on board. He asks you to recommend something as a gift for his wife.

1) Is there anything I can do for you, Sir? / Can I help you? / What can I do for you?

2) We have a wide selection on board, such as perfume, bags, silk scarves and accessories.

3) How about this one? The color is very bright.

4) Twenty five US dollars.

5) I'm sorry, Sir. We don't accept it. You have to pay in cash or by credit card.

5. Fill in the blanks in the following sentences with the words given below. Change the form where necessary.

1) currency   2) description   3) purchase   4) check   5) exclusive

6) change   7) display   8) attractive   9) cipher   10) discount

6. Complete the paragraph with the correct word in the box.

1) begin   2) available   3) discover   4) brands   5) board

6) purchase   7) contact   8) currencies   9) accepted   10) conclude

Unit 10　Transfer Service

1. Choose the correct translations in column B to match with column A.

a. 3)　　　　　b. 6)　　　　　c. 8)　　　　　d. 9)　　　　　e. 7)

f. 5)　　　　　g. 10)　　　　　h. 2)　　　　　i. 1)　　　　　j. 4)

2. Translate the following sentences into English.

1) Please hurry up. There're only thirty minutes left for your connecting flight.

2) The aircraft will go via Chongqing. The whole trip will last about five hours.

3) Passengers should prepare airline ticket and ID card for security check.

4) May I know your departure time of your connecting flight?

5) You may leave your luggage on the plane but take valuables with you.

6) Excuse me, Sir. I am your concierge agent so I'll bring you to the boarding gate.

7) The plane delayed arrival. I'm afraid. I will miss my connecting flight to Shanghai.

8) We are extremely sorry for any inconvenience caused to you. Shanghai Hongqiao International Airport has been closed due to the heavy thunderstorm, so we have to land at Hangzhou International Airport.

9) Don't worry. We'll offer you free accommodation and try to arrange you on the earliest plane to New York.

10) If you have a connecting flight, you'll have to go to the domestic terminal after you have declared customs.

3. Translate the following sentences into Chinese.

1) 你能告诉我要在临时机场停留多久吗？

2) 已经过了20分钟了，我们的飞机为什么还没有起飞？

3) 我们还要等多久？我要在北京转机，起飞延误的话会影响我接下来的转机。

4) 为什么我们要在广州白云国际机场降落？我们的目的地不是深圳机场吗？

5) 我不能确定什么时候回国，所以买了到纽约的机动机票。

6) 下机后你去国内候机楼，它就挨着国际候机楼。

7) 先生，您好，登机前您还有些时间，您愿不愿意在茶点室休息一下？

8) 下机后您可以通过登机桥或摆渡车到达候机大厅。

9) 您最好到大厅的转机柜台核实一下，他们会帮助您的。

10) 如果您继续乘坐本次航班，可以把手提行李放在机舱上，但是贵重的物品和文件要随身携带。

4. Suppose you are a flight attendant. A foreign passenger doesn't know how to go through the transit formalities to Kunming. She asks for your help.

1) Have you made a reservation for the flight to Kunming?

2) What's your flight number? What's the departure time?

3) Oh, you have to go to the domestic terminal after you have declared customs. It's just beside the international terminal.

4) Please follow the sign or ask the airport clerk who'll be able to help you.

5) It's my pleasure.

5. Fill in the blanks in the following sentences with the words given below. Change the form where necessary.

1) claim   2) disembark   3) formality   4) obtain   5) spare

6) destination 7) reserve   8) transfer   9) domestic   10) reconfirm

6. Complete the paragraph with the correct word in the box.

1) temperature 2) fuel   3) stop   4) disembark   5) claim

6) connection 7) departure   8) obtain   9) leave   10) valuables

Unit 11   Customs, Immigration and Quarantine

1. Choose the correct translations in column B to match with column A.

a. 8)   b. 7)   c. 10)   d. 2)   e. 6)

f. 1)   g. 3)   h. 4)   i. 5)   j. 9)

2. Translate the following sentences into English.

1) I believe you have to pay a duty of two hundred dollars.

2) Please fill in the Customs Declaration Form and sign your name here.

3) What's the purpose of your visit to America?

4) Please give this Health Certificate to that officer at the exit.

5) How long are you going to stay in Canada?

6) How much money do you have with you?

7) May I see your ticket and passport, please?

8) Excuse me, Madam. Do you have any difficulties in filling these forms?

9) Excuse me. Must I finish filling out the CIQ forms before landing?

10) In order to save the time of going through the formalities in the airport, you'd better complete the forms on board.

3. Translate the following sentences into Chinese.

1) 我带了一部苹果 7 手机, 需要申报吗?

2) 我不懂英语, 您能帮我填吗?

3) 打扰一下, 先生, 您能告诉我都什么东西需要报关吗?

4) 行李传送带上没找到我的包呀。

5) 打扰一下, 我还没有入境登记表, 您能给我一份吗?

6）请准备好护照和手提行李以备检查。

7）请保管好您的护照，将这张申报卡交给出口处的官员。

8）我想这儿您弄错了。这个物品的型号和申报单上写的不一样。

9）您能告诉我一下，到美国我可以带多少支免税香烟吗？

10）如果您还有其他不明白的地方，请仔细阅读申报单背面的报关物品目录。

4. Suppose you are a flight attendant. Now you are distributing CIQ to every passenger before the flight gets to its destination. Passengers ask you some questions.

1）You'd better do so in order to save your time after arriving at the airport.

2）You need to fill out your name, date of birth, airline No. , occupation, nationality, the purpose of your trip etc.

3）No problem. But you need tell me your information.

4）Well, let's fill in the forms.

5）It's our duty to serve you well.

5. Fill in the blanks in the following sentences with the words given below. Change the form where necessary.

1）submitted 2）exceed 3）refer 4）customs 5）necessity

6）distribute 7）express 8）possession 9）declare 10）dairy

6. Complete the paragraph with the correct word in the box.

1）passengers 2）forms 3）note 4）provide 5）address

6）complete 7）declaration 8）need 9）hesitate 10）understanding

Unit 12　Pre-arrival and Post-arrival

1. Choose the correct translations in column B to match with column A.

a. 7）　　b. 4）　　c. 9）　　d. 10）　　e. 5）

f. 3）　　g. 6）　　h. 1）　　i. 8）　　j. 2）

2. Translate the following sentences into English.

1）Our plane is ready to land now. For your safety, please keep your seat belt fastened.

2）We regret to inform you that we have to divert to land at Tianjing Airport due to the heavy fog in Beijing.

3）Your checked baggage has to be claimed at the Baggage Claim Area.

4）Thank you for flying with us and hope to have the pleasure of meeting with you again.

5）If you have a connecting flight, you'll have to go to the domestic terminal after you declare them.

6）We'd like to thank you for your support and cooperation during this flight.

7) We will be landing at Hong Kong International Airport in about 20 minutes.

8) It is sunny at the destination airport. The ground temperature is 25 degree Centigrade.

9) Excuse me. Sir. Is there any clear sign on your suitcase? We will try our best to look for it.

10) If your suitcase is oversized or irregular, you can go to that counter to find it.

3. Translate the following sentences into Chinese.

1) 我将在上海作短暂停留, 你能给我点建议去做些什么吗?

2) 飞机什么时候起飞? 有其他变化吗?

3) 我在如家酒店预订了房间。你能告诉我在哪儿吗?

4) 到达后乘摆渡车很方便吗?

5) 你能告诉我目的地机场的天气情况吗?

6) 我们对此很抱歉。行李到达后, 我们会尽快与您取得联系并送到您的指定地点。

7) 所有的行李都送出来了。每个人都取了他们的行李出去了。

8) 女士您好, 我没找到我的行李, 您能帮我查一下吗?

9) 据我所知, 没有直达的公共汽车去那里。您可以到候机楼外乘坐出租车。

10) 飞机已经停稳, 请带好您的随身物品下机。

4. Suppose you are a flight attendant. The plane has come to a complete stop. You are busy helping passengers with their baggage.

1) You may disembark in the front or back door.

2) You may take the ferry bus. It'll take you to the arrival hall.

3) No, it is free.

4) When you arrive, you will see the signs pointing to the Baggage Claim Area. You may get your checked baggage there.

5) Not at all. Have a nice trip.

5. Fill in the blanks in the following sentences with the words given below. Change the form where necessary.

1) grateful   2) support   3) approximated 4) obliged   5) hired

6) utmost   7) terminus   8) opportunity   9) limousine   10) additional

6. Complete the paragraph with the correct word in the box.

1) sunny   2) prepare   3) return   4) tray   5) fastened

6) devices   7) remind   8) disembark   9) behalf   10) understanding